Journey to the Soul

Kabbalah's Pathway for Your Present and Future

Jonathan M. Case

Outskirts Press, Inc.
Denver, Colorado

Journey to the Soul
Kabbalah's Pathway for Your Present and Future
All Rights Reserved.
Copyright © 2008 Jonathan M. Case
V3.0

Outskirts Press, Inc.
http://www.outskirtspress.com

ISBN: 978-1-4327-1957-9

Outskirts Press and the "OP" logo are trademarks belonging to Outskirts Press, Inc.

For Rivke, with fondness and appreciation, and a never-ending spring of love:

The winter is past
The rains are over.
They are gone.
Blossoms have appeared in the land.
Song of Songs 2:11-12

A few principles I have gleaned from life.

1. Some of my most powerful growth experiences have also been the most painful.
2. I know little and understand less.

For the innumerable teachers who have taught me, thank you. Knowledge has often come from the most unlikely sources. From the clerk at the checkout counter whose wisdom has often jarred me out an emotional stupor to the profound teachings of one of the greatest minds of our time, Louis Jacobs, may his memory be as a blessing, I am indebted.

To my dearest friends, Neal Rasiman, David Teague and Lillian Silberstein I can only say a humble word of thanks for all your love and support. My trusted advisors and companions Barry Lee and Jim Audlin (Distant Eagle) have given me great, incalculable gifts.

I could never express the depth of my gratitude for the bottomless love of a mother whose greatest gifts to me were an infatuation with the seashore, sunshine and an endless well of hope and to a father who tenaciously clung to youth and laughter. These tools have enabled me to find rays of light even on the darkest nights.

For the opportunities afforded by my breath, I thank my Creator. Your Voice has strengthened my life and steadied my journey. Even when You are silent echoes of past meetings fill me.

To my children Eliahu, Penina and Miriam; may your aspirations be tinged with zeal and enthusiasm so that you find joy in the actions of your hands. May your eyes seek and find the goodness that inheres in every being. May you be blessed with a selective memory that allows forgiveness from past hurts. May you always love yourselves while giving and receiving ample love from others. May your world be kinder than that of past generations and may the word of our God be found on your lips.

Within every human being there is a wellspring of power that lies dormant. Just beneath the skein of the face that we present to the world, that strength patiently bides its time, hoping and waiting for release. This great untapped potential waits. We know it is there. Even in our darkest moments, we have suspected that there is far more to life, and to us, than we have acknowledged. At times, we have felt a power move within us that is unnamable.

"In the midst of winter I finally learned that there was in me an invincible summer." -Albert Camus

Table of Contents

Foreword 1
An Introduction 3

Section One: Finding the Missing 13
The Problem, the Path and the Preparation
1. **The Beginning of the Journey.** A question of where we start. How long is the road? Where do I begin? 15
2. **Bored. Is This Really Me?** An examination of things we consider to be most important in life. Why don't these critical items deliver the jolt of lasting satisfaction that we crave? One special person who tread this path before us and how he dealt with the big problems of life.... Discover a universe of feeling 21
3. **Caring for the Soul and Self.** Move from being insignificant toward becoming a unique treasure of God's creation. How to perceive the primal light of creation. Putting forth a deliberate movement toward making our own light. The point where heaven and earth connect. 41
4. **Forgiveness, the Path of Light and Darkness.** If life is an ocean, how do we manage to float instead of sink and drown? Leaden weights attached to our souls and can so encumber our journey through life that we might not "make it". 57
5. **A Reason to Be on Fire.** How to catch fire without resorting to retreating from life: even in the lowest depths of hell there can be light. What can be learned from the searing pain of loneliness? ...69
6. **The Angry Client (at times known as a brooding neighbor, the perennially upset relative, human roadblock, the noxious person...a.k.a. your nemesis).** What do we see with our eyes? Reality? Or do we only see what we are predisposed to see? What hurts me may be real without my consent. We can validate our life in an instant. 81
7. **The Point Where Heaven and Earth Converge.** Trying to locate the place called Eden. Heaven and earth are mirror images of one another. If God is "one," what are we? 97

8. **Expectations: Your Worst Enemy**. The story of Job. Why do we expect not to suffer? Are gifts presents or are they curses because of what comes with them? Can other people be unique too? Or must everyone be equal?..105

9. **You and God**. The place where real connection begins. Does God pray? An analysis of the tale of Noah and his subsequent generations. Does the tale of "Noah and his generations" have anything to teach us? Or is it just a quaint story?...................117

10. **Nefesh**. The root of the person. How relieving yourself can initiate the path towards finding our spiritual center. The awe, wonder and joy of a tightrope walker. Sniffing the world..............125

11. **Ruach**. The memory of a flower. Perhaps it smells even more beautiful in our mind…. This aspect is created from the breath of God. The real story of the genesis of beauty. 137

12. **Neshama**. Discovering the highest level of life. The sigh that almost broke the portals of the universe. The danger of crossing over to hold the three most vital aspects of our being. 145

Section Two: A Practicum 159
The Solution

1. **Checklist for life**. A study of grass and how it impacts our soul. How to change the world knowing that it may not be real but only a metaphor. The story of an aggravated nurse and her sewing needle. Unleashing *their* potential. 161

2. **Getting up**. Take your ticket: victim or victimizer? Giver or taker? Choose one. That choice will define our day. What Oskar Schindler has to teach us..171

3. **Scheduling**. Life in the fast lane. Can I slow this process down? "You had to be there." Look..185

4. **Zeal**. The best funeral I ever attended. Expressions of devotion. Count the kinds of affection. The sadness of God. How a sacrifice becomes a knot of love. The Temple fires........................197

5. **An Ennobled Self**. A Temple of Judgment. A Temple of Righteousness. How we can be whole in a world which continually gnaws at our spirit. Arriving at the ultimate sense of being alive.............207

Section Three: **And the moral of the story is**…. 219

Foreword

Of all the addictions in which the Western culture is sinking, I think the most prevalent is the one that infects its victims with the belief that they are experts on all subjects.

Everyone has an opinion on every subject of public interest, and is all too willing to share it. Never mind the fact that most people don't know the facts in the matter, never mind that their views were shaped by other self-appointed opinion-givers in the media. You name the celebrity, everyone has a view on that person's mental state, ethics, and talent. You name the issue, everyone has a view on how it should be solved.

I'm sure you've noticed how when you have a difficult issue, or are facing something serious – divorce, the birth of a child, surgery, financial difficulties – many of your friends will chime in with, "Well, when *I*..." and tell you what you should do. Everybody's an expert!

Take the self-help field. At your local bookstore you'll find racks of these books each one promising to change your life for the better. On radio and television, dozens of sage mystics pass out wise-sounding platitudes to absolute strangers.

Of course, all of their prescriptions for success, for wealth, for popularity, for health are different, often conflicting – but let that not be an impediment, since by promoting themselves these people are sure to find success, wealth, and popularity in the marketplace.

Save your money. Gimmicks are for guppies. Platitudes are for platypuses. The truth about how to live a truly good life is never slicked out in fancy phrases and pretty pronouncements.

Thank Goodness – that is, the Goodness who created us and who loves us – that Rabbi Jonathan Case has laid out for us this truth, the truth of what *does* promise a good life. And he has done so in eloquent, engaging writing. Throw the self-help books out. Forget the workshops and the lectures and the glib sophistry on morning television. Read this book with thoughtful care, think about what it is saying, and you will find for yourself the good, true, simple answers that will indeed make life what it should be.

Will Rabbi Case's teaching make you rich? Nope. Will his book make you popular? Not likely. Will it make you lose weight? Only if you carry fifty copies of it for ten miles every day.

But it will help you understand the simple beauty of living peacefully with yourself and others. For that I am eternally grateful.

The Rev. James David Audlin
author of *Circle of Life*

An Introduction

A tale.

A trembling disciple approached his Master, Reb Shmelke. Reb Shemlke was one of *them*, the holy ones.

Shmelke's reputation was so well-known that the spiritually hungry would travel for hundreds of miles just to spend one single Sabbath of their life with him. When he prayed, the Master's body would convulse with the languishing emotions of five thousand years; and when the Master sang, every fiber of his being vibrated to the melody that seemed to emerge from everywhere and nowhere.

Rumors about the holy teacher abounded. People often said that the Master even conversed with the ancient ones, long dead. To study under such a sage meant observing his every movement; the way he ate, dressed, prayed, put on his shoes. Every action Reb Shmelke performed had meaning and it was up to the student to listen, observe and then follow.

Over the course of many years of watching and imitating the saintly teacher, observing his customs and absorbing teachings, the disciple saw what an impoverished life he lived. 'Why?' he wondered. The holy Master could have anything he wanted. Followers of Reb Shmelke would go to any ends to meet the needs of their venerated teacher. And still the Master chose to live an ascetic life, refusing to rise above being a pauper. Nothing would be withheld, if only he were to ask. Hesitating, the student approached Reb Shmelke trying to frame the embarrassing question:

"You are very poor, my Master. And still you thank God for His many gifts to you. Aren't you deceiving yourself? Or worse, lying to God?"

The Sage smiled and responded, "No. You see, for me, poverty is what I need."

What are you looking for? In the journey of your life, what stands out as the objects you pursue? Fill in the following phrase: "I am ____ years old. What does my life stand for? What have I accomplished in my years that defines me? In all these years I have lived where have I focused my energies? What have I devoted most of my hours to? Who am I?"

If this is too difficult to answer, let us try another approach: Walk into your own home like stranger and gaze around. What do you see? What do the surroundings say about you? Look at the objects on your mantle, the pictures on your wall, the furniture in your home. Each of these items sends out a message of your priorities. Each object represents you and says something about your values.

Each house possesses a voice which conveys its message to every visitor that traffics through its doors. The house that we live in sends out a powerful, unequivocal message about who lives there. What does your house say about you? Are you satisfied with it? Are you satisfied with your life? Are you happy with the things in which you have invested countless hours and immeasurable energy?

People seek many things during the span of their years. Often these priorities change as we mature. Among the priorities might be wealth, renown, respect, knowledge, prowess. Which of these (or all) do you seek? Our wants may be many, but *what are our needs*? The question which frames and responds to the ultimate journey and yearning of the soul is; what do you need?

The road to wholeness is obtained by living a life that is genuine and true to our soul. Reb Shmelke, a wise man, was aware that his soul was maintained and satisfied by keeping his present lifestyle, even though it meant living in poverty. Anything else would have corrupted or sent him hurtling in a different direction. He knew what made him whole and it was not riches or self-aggrandizement.

The inner world, Shmelke knew, is influenced by what lies outside of it. Reb Shmelke had the balance he needed. 'What else do I need?' Shmelke must have asked himself. With this wisdom guiding him, the Master knew the correct answer. Nothing. More wealth, more food, more accumulated possessions were not going to make

Shmelke more happy. On the contrary, riches would only impoverish the holy man; it would upset the balance.

This book is about finding what you need. It is a roadmap to find our self. Just as Reb Shmelke knew what made him whole, what would it be worth to find what would make you truly happy? Many people devote endless hours devouring rich tomes and libraries of self-help books in their quest for happiness. The underlying premise of this book is that you do not have to give up all worldly possessions or move to an *ashram* to find contentment. The quest for joy does not necessarily mean seeking a better job or finding a more appreciative spouse. Can you find meaning in your life now? As it is.

The word *Kabbalah* means 'reception'. The mystic tradition exists and is within our reach. All that remains to gather the kernels of this wisdom, to absorb the Kabbalah, is to learn how to be open enough to receive it. It is already there waiting for us to take it. Like radio waves, transmissions abound; they circle around us even now. Our task is to have our antennae extended and attuned so that we can hear them. Kabbalah is about opening up our minds and souls to receive what is patiently waiting for us. One of the primary goals of this book is to create an awareness of things not seen but nonetheless present.

The real change we need to make is a shift in perception. The world will not change to suit our desires. In fact, as we will soon learn, it *must* not change to meet our desires. Everything is exactly as it needs to be for us to begin the most dramatic shift of our life. What we require is the equipment, the inner tools, with which to change our relationship with our environment into something more compelling and meaningful. A new understanding.

An extraordinarily wise man named Maimonides who informed and enlightened the Arab, Jewish and Christian communities for centuries, made the following observation. "I believe that it is not fitting to walk in the orchard unless one has filled oneself with bread and meat. And that bread and meat is the knowledge of what is forbidden and what is allowed."

The "orchard" of which Maimonides speaks is the place where contentment can be found. Reb Shmelke and other vitally alive people lived in the orchard. Entering into that domain is the goal of every spiritually aware being and exists for all people cutting across continents, skin hues and belief systems. We all harbor the desire to find this Eden; the orchard where the richness of existence makes us feel truly alive. That is why every civilization has its myths about a place of perfection which was once hidden until humankind forfeited its rights to that Garden.

Maimondes discloses that not only does this orchard exist, it is still accessible. We may have been exiled from the physical place but the spiritual Eden still is open and accessible. Yet in order to gain access to the orchard we must be willing to learn how to prepare ourselves to enter into that new/old realm. It is 'old' because it has existed since the inception of the universe. The orchard is as ancient as the earth itself. It is 'new' because we cannot get there through incantations or riding on the crest created by our forebears. It becomes 'new' because in the midst of discovering it for ourselves we are re-created. In the orchard are the secrets that every person knows exists and longs to find. Once we find the portal that opens up to that place of contentment, it is new to us.

The fact that you are reading this book is an indication that you know, or at least you want to believe, that such a place exists. It may even mean more than that. It might indicate that you desire the full, complete sense of being alive that comes from entering the orchard. Perhaps the largest, most difficult segment of your journey has already commenced (and succeeded!) You already recognize the critical importance of finding and opening the door to the orchard -- and wanting to enter and eat.

The bread and meat, mentioned by Maimonides, are the necessary elements that will sustain us throughout the journey. Of course, the sage does not mean bread and meat literally. Bread represents earth. As wheat grows from the ground it absorbs all the basic trace elements found in the world. All the minerals of the ground are vital to the essence of the wheat. The earth is the sustaining force as all growth emerges from it. In a sense, bread then is representative of the created universe; a microcosm of all that exists.

Meat, while being sustained by the earth, also sustains the earth. Animals feed from the ground to gain nourishment. They only live because the earth lives. Paradoxically, the earth is replenished by the animal life that feeds on it. The excrement, the leavings and ultimately the animal itself revitalizes the nutrients in the soil. The two-- bread and meat-- are in a symbiotic relationship. One exists for the other. In other words, these two disparate elements are really one whole.

Why does Maimonides tell us that we need this bread and meat in order to gain entry tot the mystic orchard? Just as one would not think of going on a long hike without adequate provisions, so it is with the greatest journey of life. What do we need when we enter the orchard? We need the things that will sustain us on our trek, enable us to stay on the right path. Bread and meat are the sustaining forces that bind us to the universe and keep our feet on the path towards our ultimate destination. Both are needed. Both are necessary. We will explore in the coming chapters how to access the bread and meat for our journey. For now, it is important to remember that these provisions not only keep us alive, they provide direction. With our bread and meat secured in our storehouses, we possess what we need to be complete and satisfied. Having them is a kind of knowledge that informs our life's journey. We are whole and ready to travel the road of light. The Kabbalah contains the elements of the bread and meat. It tells us how to access these necessary ingredients and carry them as we enter into the orchard.

In the process of preparing for the journey towards the orchard, we gain a framework in which to understand the outer cosmos as well as the mirror inner image. *Kabbalah is not just a way of thinking, it is a way of acting and behavior.* It means living in harmony with our soul. Kabbalah is outward --in telling us how we must live --and inward --in giving us clues in how to approach or days. It is making the inner world mesh with what happens to us on the road of life.

Much of what we learn through the way others live their lives, misdirects us. Our society seeks the easy path. We want to know how to lose weight without extensive dieting or exercise. Advertisements profess their ability to teach perfect speech by listening to cassettes/cd's. We demand knowledge in quick bites. Entrepreneurs have learned that to sell their wares they must be able to claim that almost no effort is required by the purchaser. "No assembly required" is the best indication of a salable item.

The proliferation of the "How to…for Dummies" series attests to our desire to acquire things effortlessly. Kabbalah and most religions do not agree with this modern philosophy. Instead, they demand attention to details. It is the little stuff, the details, which is actually quite large and meaningful while the big stuff tends to be fleeting in both meaning and joy.

Jonathan M. Case

Maimonides - philosopher, sage, leader and doctor -was a man on a level with Leonardo daVinci. Living in the twelfth century, he was a polyglot of languages, proficient in Arabic, Spanish, Aramaic, and Hebrew among others. To this day Jewish physicians swear an oath to protect and heal that was first crafted by this man long ago.

Maimonides makes another observation: He says that while studying the "work of the chariot" is lofty, the small subjects of life come first. The far-seeing teacher brings us back to the Bible.

Remember the tale of Elijah? Eons ago lived a fearless, unique man whose name still brings awe and deep reverence. Elijah stood before kings and confronted them with uncomfortable truths. He challenged the ultimate human authorities, excoriating them for their misdeeds, and did not flinch from this task. Elijah was a man who was "true" to his soul; he was not conflicted about his life's path.

As His gifted prophet, God gave Elijah something wondrous, beyond words, when his earthly mission came to an end. At the moment he was ready to leave the world, Elijah was given a matchless gift rendered to no other human being before or after, an end that had no ending. The gift was life that held no death. When Elijah's "time" approached, God sent to earth a flaming chariot to escort the prophet to heaven. The prophet stepped into the heaven-sent fiery blaze and it carried him upward. Was it really a chariot? If so, what is the meaning of this vehicle? If it was not a chariot, then what was it? What does this enigmatic story mean?

The "work of the chariot", according to Maimonides, is esotericism, the discovery and contemplation of the greatest mystery of life. The tale of Elijah goes well beyond the boundaries of this story of long ago. It whispers to us that the chariot was not intended for Elijah alone. That whisper tells us that it is available to anyone who possesses the keys to apprehend its meaning. It is that chariot which beckons those who seek enlightenment. Those who have read the tale of the great prophet of biblical lore know that Elijah's soul was tied to God. Elijah had a rich relationship with the One. Yet, warns Maimonides, even Elijah, so beloved of God, did not merit to even look at the "chariot" until he first understood a blade of grass. The small stuff comes before the large.

The Zohar, the basic textbook of Kabbalah, states: "Because there is a rose there is a rose." What the Zohar subtly wants us to

10

learn is that what we apprehend is reality. In other words, if we understand that there is a rose, the rose will be there. If we do not wish to see it, it does not exist. Our receptivity to the existence and beauty of the rose depends upon us, not the rose. Kabbalah wants to open our minds to the existence of the universe and then open our hearts to listen on a different level.

Something is definitely askew when a person will strive to reach God, taking courses in mysticism and studying with holy teachers, while taking medicine to lower their blood pressure. I know a man who has worked for years to refine his ability to meditate on higher and higher levels. He goes on regular retreats and spends hours churning over mantras. When he goes home, he is transformed; he degenerates to a wreck. His children do not appreciate his gentle nature and calm demeanor. They eat him alive. After a few minutes at home, he is screaming louder than the heavy metal music his son plays. First things first. This book is about life as it is, maybe not as we have imagined it to be. It is not a book that renders the world in incomprehensible terms, beyond our means. **Journey to the Soul** is for our life.

The Kabbalistic bent to this book is one which uses ancient approaches to make sense of our time. It is concerned with the little things: relationships, words, time, meetings, cutting the deal. From the universe of the mundane, Kabbalah insists, we can become whole. Elevating the meaning of every day life enables us to traverse to higher spheres. It, like all things, is a process.

This journey then is about finding the bread and meat of existence. It is about locating what we need in order to be us. There are no videos to purchase; no diet pills or mysterious tomes leading us to that goal. We have been gifted with all that we need for the journey. Now like the holy master, Reb Shmelke, we must find what we need.

A cautionary note: it is a simple task to remove any one of these statements from context or ignore significant steps of the process. A genuine desire for holiness is not just an ephemeral spiritual journey but a deep welling of desire to follow the right path. The striving to meet God must be accompanied by the equally strong desire to live a good life. Clearly stated, this holy pathway must be joined with a genuine desire to be better people by behaving morally, going out of our way to be kind and good.

All journeys must start at the beginning. This one is no different. Kabbalah is so vast that it is not possible to maneuver through all its great depths. That is why this book is the start, certainly not the total knowledge of this venerable mystic tradition, of the personal journey which is accomplished in a series of long, determined steps.

One more idea before we begin. An instruction. All soulful journeys are not events that can be viewed as a passenger. We do not witness them as a spectator through a plate-glass window in our lives, taking copious notes for absorption and future reference. We are not the passenger, we are not even the conductor; we are the train. To that end, at the conclusion of each chapter is a summation of where we have traveled. It will be short, simply a reminder. The purpose of this summation is for learning and integration. Review that passage and then try to consciously live it before moving on to the next segment of the journey.

All that remains now is to unpack this knowledge then begin to use it...

Section One:
The Problem, The Path
and The Preparation

Chapter 1

The Beginning of the Journey

Listen to the tale: he is running for his life. In the stillness of a universe where no sound can be heard, Jacob's ears are only attuned to the rhythmic plodding of his feet on the parched earth. He is running. Jacob's heart is beating so irregularly and ferociously that it feels like it might collapse on itself any moment. With each gulp of breath comes the slicing pain of the prolonged exhalation, anxious for the next breath to sustain him a bit longer on the tortuous journey. And then there is the unbearable agony of being hounded, hated and having to live the rest of his life in exile.

When the father hears of the deceit, he will be unforgiving. How could it be otherwise? Jacob has lied to his father. Impersonating his brother Esau, Jacob stole away before the ruse could be unmasked and Jacob shamed. The relationship between father and son is forever broken. Mother used him. Again! How could he ever face her after this? (Little does Jacob know that by the time he returns home after his years of running, she will long be dead. He will never see her face again.) And the fierceness of his brother's anger will be relentless.

Jacob's twin is the anti-hero. Esau is brazen, full of bravado and ire and even now, miles away, Jacob can hear Esau's wild howls of anguish. Esau will become the slayer. Jacob knows his life has lost all meaning. He will spend the remainder of his days hiding; wondering when Esau will finally catch up and have his long-wanted revenge.

Once upon a time Jacob was secure; life provided everything he required. Favorite of his mother, a precocious learner, scion of the land's most wealthy family, Jacob's life had almost a story-book quality to it. Why then did this all have to happen? What was the reason that all had gone awry in a few hours? Why did he ever think he could come away richer from such lies and deception?? Now, beyond hope, as his legs propel him aimlessly into the dark weave of night when it becomes impossible for him to travel any further, Jacob's heart is so heavy that he feels utterly barren, empty of all emotion. Jacob is about ready to surrender every ideal, hope and vision he ever held. This may be the last night of his life.

Finally, with a stone for a pillow, Jacob sleeps. He dreams of ladders and angels. He dreams of a pathway that climbs to the highest height. He witnesses the place where heaven and earth touch. Awake with a promise, he utters, "God is in this place and I. I never knew." *Genesis 28*

Jacob is no more. The man who would have spent the remaining years of his life looking over his shoulder has disappeared. Jacob has glimpsed the expanse of the cosmos, he has experienced the Ineffable and will never be the same. From the merciless and unforgiving pit of death, Jacob is reborn.

Does Jacob's tale resonate with your life experience? Are parts of the story so familiar that you could almost substitute your name for Jacob's? Like Jacob, most of us will endure such dark journeys in our life. At these moments, hope is absent. No light can penetrate the thick veil of blankness that envelopes and threatens to wring out our last breath. These are times that are life changing. From this empty night of despair can emerge a reborn self.

Are you tentative as you begin this journey? Nervous and apprehensive like father Jacob as he set out from all that was safe and known? Even if we do not like the life we are in, the seeming danger inherent in moving out of inertia can paralyze us. We often do nothing even when a change is demanded. That we require an Esau to relentlessly pursue us before we finally make a move – or tragically surrender our self rather than face the change- is a shame, a tragedy. Sometimes, it can even be the cause of a wasted life.

So much of what we hear about Kabbalah is either shrouded in mystery or contradiction. On the one hand, actors and actresses, celebrities of the moment, have publicly glommed onto Kabbalah to enrich their lives. Sporting red strings and gulping down holy water, they claim to have found *it*. On the other hand, old masters schooled in ancient ways have spent their lives plowing through difficult and wizened texts. Steeped in lore and practice, full of knowledge, these venerable Kabbalists attempt to penetrate the underpinnings of existence. They, who understand time as unfettered by any boundary, are able to access other universes. So which is the real Kabbalah? The fad *du jour* or the path of the ancients?

Kabbalah is a unique age-old Jewish path of relationships, both vertical and horizontal. Starting with the vertical connection, Kabbalah is a particular way of relating to the Divine One. It demands complete focus and dedication to the Almighty. Indicating practices and rites that span millennia, Kabbalah seeks to use the physical world as a vehicle to apprehend that which transcends the media of language and leaves the traveler gasping in awe. In other words, the first of Kabbalah's purposes is to have a deep connection with God; one which involves the utter desire to see the Divine Face, to experience the rapture of having glimpsed limitless power and being overwhelmed by its power and answer to life's ultimate question. And what is that question?

The question starts out with, 'Why am I alive?' There is a presumption, though, or at least a hope, that there is a reason why we live and die. Our life cannot be just an accident. It must not be meaningless. There must be a reason for our life. At the same time, we want to know if there is an explanation for why we suffer. Deep inside we know there is a purpose to our life, our pain, our love. We long for Jacob's dream/vision leading him to an absolute understanding. The journey of our life, and the ultimate question, is to uncover those answers.

Using holy words, incantations, practices and an almost total abnegation of self, the Kabbalist psychically rises beyond the belt holding the rest of us to earth. A great teacher who had a remarkable effect on my early career, Lionel Blue, once remarked that most peo-

17

ple do not regularly attend any religious house of worship. "Why?" he rhetorically asked, knowing full well the answer he was seeking. "They cannot bring themselves to come because they have one plaguing thought: "What if I pray to God and He actually responds?' The possibility that God might actually answer our prayers is too terrifying to most people, Blue stated. The Kabbalist does not fear that *it might work;* his life is devoted to that end.

The second connective tissue, a horizontal line, is complementary to the vertical. Horizontally, life is comprised of relationships with the physical realm. The way we meet people, treat them, the way we look at trees and view the earth; how we breathe and how family constellations are interwoven with our lives are all components of the horizontal connection. Kabbalah informs the way we behave and the meaning we take from every moment. It infuses each meeting (or potential meeting) with meaning and hope. Some times, the Kabbalist knows, God speaks to us directly and other times He uses people as His mouthpiece. Therefore, every human interaction is potentially a holy encounter.

Kabbalah prepares the initiate to open avenues and channels of the self which have been bolted shut or ignored for so long that they have lost their voice and are relegated to the dark places of the mind. Opening them is no simple task. They have been shut for so long that every part of our being resists opening those doors. We are fearful of change; of peering into neglected corners of our self. Oft times it is infinitely more convenient and safe, to stay where you are: stuck.

To venture into unknown regions requires a resolute decision of great courageousness. Kabbalah recognizes that each human has an unending potential for mastery. With every new level achieved comes a larger universe pulsating with possibility. A new level then appears that is even more vast than the previous one. It is almost like unfolding a map. At first it appears to be a small rectangle. Yet, as we slowly unfold the map we become aware of more and more that we did not know existed.

This is what Jacob meant when he proclaimed, "God is in this Place and I....I never knew." Life appeared to him to be without meaning: it was vapid; virtually worthless if everything could be distilled to blessing and curse, profit and loss. When his eyes perceived Heaven, Jacob saw what he knew in his heart always existed but could not grasp. What he saw was an expanse that raced out toward infinity. Once his mind was open and prepared, Jacob's perception was unlocked. What his visions enabled him to see was full of absolute awe that made him gasp with wonder when he witnessed the breadth of Self and Other. Just as he would never be the same, we have a chance as well. The opportunity to change the focus, direction and import of life is within our reach. This is where we begin *our* journey....

Chapter 2

Bored. Is This Really Me?

"Give me a sense of why I am alive. Sometimes it all seems so futile.... Yet the fact that I am here must indicate some purpose for my existence...if that is so, what is that purpose?"

The Backdrop

One of the most famous photographs of the civil rights era captures a young black girl, Elizabeth Eckford. The picture reveals a terrifying scene. Clutching books fiercely next to her chest for protection, the teenager Eckford is walking in front of another student whose face is filled with hate and rage. This white tormentor stands menacingly at the back of Elizabeth; mouth wide shouting, screaming with growing frenzy. The photograph is a snapshot of a single moment forever remembered on September 4, 1957 as Elizabeth Eckford attempted to enter her new school for the first time in Little Rock, Arkansas.

Elizabeth's story actually began a few years before the day when the photograph was snapped. The Supreme Court was challenged to determine whether a "separate but equal" school system afforded black and white students the same opportunity for learning and growth. Thanks to the dogged pursuit by the NAACP to prove the system skewed, the Supreme Court ultimately ruled in 1954 that black students relegated to a *blacks only* system suffered. There was no parity in a separate education. The Supreme Court set its ruling demanding that schools integrate their students. The idea that a separate school could be equal was wrong.

Arkansas was strident in its refusal to recognize and adhere to the Supreme Court's decision. On one side were students and parents who desperately wanted the best education possible. A solid foundation would lead to a life of opportunity based on merit, not skin color. At risk was not just the present but the future lives of these students. On the other side of the argument was a vast majority of frightened people. They were *very* scared. Hadn't the Governor, Orval Faubus, declared that no such integration, mixing of the races, should take place? The fate of the children of Arkansas was being planned by some dispassionate heads in Washington. Those Judges did not have kids in Arkansas schools! What right did they have to place their children's future in jeopardy?

President Eisenhower felt the pressure in Washington. He used his weight to enforce the decision of the nation's highest court. Eisenhower drew upon the authority of his office and persuasive skills to convince the state to abide by the ruling by the Court. Faubus remained unmoved. Gripped by fear that would allow black students to be educated alongside white students, the Governor ordered the Arkansas National Guard to physically intervene and prevent Elizabeth and other black teenagers from attending Little Rock Central High School on the first day of school, September 3. Faubus publicly announced this defiant act the night before school was to begin.

Under the organizing talents of Daisy Bates, the "Little Rock Nine" were prepared for whatever might happen on the first day. Of all the potential students who could attend Little Rock Central, only nine sets of parents were willing to expose their children to such danger. In numbers, Daisy Bates reasoned, there would be strength. Even if there were only nine students, they would march into the High School as one body. Bates planned for all students to enter the school together.

Complications developed and Daisy decided that the plans would have to be postponed until Wednesday. So the evening before the start of school, after the governor's venomous speech, Daisy tried to contact each of the students so she could tell them to wait until Wednesday, the second day of school, so that she could go with them.

Elizabeth Eckford's family did not have a phone. She never received the message. Elizabeth showed up for school that day. Alone.

That morning as fifteen-year-old Elizabeth Eckford approached the school clutching her books, she heard voices. "They're here! The niggers are coming!" Elizabeth bravely continued to walk the gantlet. She was spat upon, cursed, jeered with every step. All she wanted to was to get to the safety of the school. But Governor Faubus had done his best to ensure that would not happen. The National Guard was positioned around the school, forming an impenetrable ring around Little Rock Central. Every time Elizabeth tried to get by them, the guardsmen crossed their bayonets so she could not pass; all the while, epithets and jeers continued to be hurled at her. Elizabeth stopped and stood, quietly trembling, when she realized the situation was hopeless. Then turned to walk back to the bus stop, powerless to stop the barrage. "Get her! Lynch her!" The boys were screaming, "Go home you bastard of a black bitch!" She thought she heard somebody say, "Get a rope and drag her over to this tree." Disguising her pain behind dark glasses, this single picture captures a revealing moment.

For eighteen long days, President Dwight Eisenhower tried to reason with Faubus and convince him that it was for the good of the nation that the children be allowed to attend the school. Finally, on September 24, President Eisenhower felt compelled to appear on television and declare, "Our enemies are gloating over this incident and using it everywhere to misrepresent our whole nation. We are portrayed as a violator of those standards which the peoples of the world united to proclaim in the Charter of the United Nations." The President was forced to send in federal troops.

The path to civil rights for all Americans was a long and tortuous one that meandered in many unanticipated directions. This one photograph of a young high school girl shows how perilous and jagged that journey was. After all the pain suffered by individuals and the trauma of the entire nation, is it any surprise that one of the greatest triumphal moments in civil rights was equality in education? It was seen as the ultimate liberation!

The greatest fear of the white community in the late 1950's was that their *shared* commodity - education - would somehow limit *their* future success. It was as if they were saying, 'Our education is all that sets us apart. It provides us with a wedge, an advantage; the safety of the segregated education ensures our survival as it keeps a barrier between us and them. How can you take away that protective cordon and leave us so vulnerable? How can you allow them to share in our greatest treasure, education? What will become of us?'

In the United States, the idea that a person might be illiterate today is practically unthinkable. Unrestricted access to higher education has been the beacon of freedom for all people. It is what Elizabeth and eight others fought for. It is also what countless millions have pinned their future aspirations on: education. Our unstated belief has been that knowledge is liberation as well as opportunity. It is the key that unlocks every door.

If the twentieth century goes in recorded history as the time in which technology and inventions raced ahead at a breakneck pace; when science advanced so swiftly that only the well-read could keep up, then the underpinning of it all lies in education. Ignorance is equivalent to failure. Knowledge levels to the field so that anyone can succeed. Education, problem solving, and creativity are the venerated skills of modernity. They are the tools of success.

In the past, trades and skills were passed down through family and birth lines. The guilds, which once controlled access to the trades, were tightly controlled. They belonged to only the privileged by birth. Those fortunate enough to have the "right" parents had a promised future. Modernity, on the other hand, has devised a meritocracy not based on birthright, but by achievement. The modern day equivalent of the once powerful guild is education. Education is the modern-day equivalent of the alchemist's vision to create gold. Take enough knowledge and it can be transformed into the most powerful element on earth. Now, countless schools across America display the message "Knowledge is Power."

The tumultuous times of desegregation and forced bussing raised the ideal of education as a kind of modern Moses which could free any person from the shackles of inferiority. It would strip away all privilege, class and birthright and land opportunity in the lap of anyone hardworking enough to pursue it. With enough information we can solve any issue, bring on the messianic era.

The Question

Is this true? Does an accumulation of knowledge make us whole? Are we free now that we have universal access to higher education? We have successfully enfranchised all members of American society. Everyone has equal access to a prosperous future. Have we achieved the goal we were seeking? Was it Moses leading us to the Promised Land? Or have our educational triumphs only forestalled the inevitable question; why am I alive?

The paradox of life often belies the statement that with education comes knowledge and that is the true liberation. Closer to reality is that knowledge may work for or against us. There are times when it allows us to wield power, at times it helps us to achieve status and attain positions. Yet, the largest question remains, does it lead to a sense of deep soulful satisfaction?

The expression "ignorance is bliss" has taken on new meaning. There is a sense that the unlettered farmer may be much better off than we are. With his daily chores and hands in the earth he is not tethered to his beeper. He does not jump when the telephone rings. He is not sitting at his computer desk sending memos and faxes to clients. He does not suffer from carpal tunnel syndrome or high blood pressure.

All the college years, the earned degrees, the many years spent cultivating and honing a business have served to make us slaves to our own success. Has your learning brought with it the hoped- for answers to life? Are you happy? Are you fulfilled? Is this what life is all about? Have we found *it*? In a sense, our grandest achievements have also been our most abysmal failures.   Translation: Knowledge has become our merciless taskmaster sapping energy and time while depriving us of real opportunity to discover our soul and uncover the meaning of our life. Unrelenting, it summons us to work more hours with a diminishing sense of satisfaction.

A common myth is that when we have answers to problems, we will be "in control" and "responsible." Closer to reality is that we are not "in control" at all. The force of our life controls us instead of the other way around. The truth is also that sometimes we are not right, even if we know all the correct things to do and say. It is amazing how often we can be wrong when we are right. Anyone not living alone on a desert island knows this to be true. Knowing the correct answer does not respond to the ultimate riddle of life. It does not feed our relationships. It does not respond to the query of the soul.

On the one hand, we ask, *'If knowledge is really liberating, how come I feel so enslaved?'* *'Why am I working so hard just to maintain where I am?'* *'And why do I feel so empty at the end of the day?'* On the other hand, sometimes secure with a learned response, we find ourselves handicapped by that knowledge. We are too learned, too knowledgeable, to be caught off-guard; too educated to be surprised; too full of facts and opinions to feel unashamed awe. We have become dispassionate and detached from spontaneous joy, wonder and even sadness. In other words, we are emotionally and spiritually empty with no guide book to show us the way out.

We have become factually knowledgeable people and have discovered that those facts alone do not supply the answer we need. What have we learned? We have learned that knowledge does not mean fulfillment. It is only a means to a specific end. Education, like possessions, should direct us toward joy. It ought to provide clues for the path to wholeness. Yet it does not.

I received a call from a woman many years ago. It was not long after I had started my second pulpit. Just having arrived at the office after my morning coffee I was still a bit asleep (for me, the body functions well before the brain in the early part of the morning). Sounding to my addled brain like a noticeably pained voice, she said, "I'd like to stop by and just say hello and get acquainted…we never really met….." We scheduled an appointment for later that day.

She arrived at my office exactly at the scheduled time. Well dressed and well-spoken, the woman sat down with care and poise. She immediately launched to the heart of her concern, "I have been married for about ten years. Generally, it has been good but sometimes my husband just doesn't get it. I tell him what's on my mind. I talk to him about problems I am having in my life. Joe's response to me is always the same. He offers a quick solution. He gives me advice. He sizes up the problem and tells me what to do. He is a smart man and a good problem-solver…but he doesn't get it when I tell him *that* is not what I want!"

What she had trouble articulating (and her husband had even more difficulty understanding) was that she was looking for empathy, not answers. All he needed to do for her was to get out of the modality of responding to her problems with answers and instead just give her a hug and say "that's too bad." Does this resonate? Brought up in the milieu that believes that knowledge will liberate us, this story makes no sense. Knowledge solves problems; it does not make them.

We venerate knowledge; genuflect before the altar of empirical fact. We react to events based on our learned responses and scientific understanding. We ably apply techniques of induction, deduction and reduction, all of which makes us successful and productive workers and employers, but often failures in the ultimate enterprise, life. Above, the husband, Joe, was acting in accord with the process of reasoning and logic. In other words, he was correct...but he was not right.

Life happens. Generally speaking, this is a good thing. Too much predictability is monotonous and boring. Life brings with it unexpected twists and turns. The unseen and unknown can be exhilarating and/or terrifying. Within boundaries, doesn't something out of the ordinary excite and enthuse you? A near-miss collision that we craftily avoid might provide a jolt of adrenaline but an accident is a different matter altogether. That is sheer terror. It is fine to plan a hold-onto-your-pants-white-water-rafting trip, but it is not the way most people would choose to live their lives on a daily basis.

We seek controlled lives that are informed by our understanding of life. Life is predictable and manageable when we are adequately prepared for the journey. Once again, knowledge is the key. Yet is this enough? With our accumulated learning, are we thus prepared for life? Or do we spend clear-thinking moments wondering what we are doing on earth? Knowledge and intricate preparedness neither pads nor insulates our lives, and it does not deliver meaning.

Why am I alive?

As a pulpit minister I am ever aware of the power of ritual in our lives. Essentially, rituals fall into two categories. There are the stable and predictable rituals of the religious kind and those that people create as a response to a need. We develop rhythms or rituals to introduce order in place of chaos. That is why some people always put their shirt on before their trousers; or they put their keys in the same place or tune up their car on the same day each season; or say "God bless you" when someone sneezes even if they no longer remember why they say it. Such rituals give order and structure and allow us to feel a measure of control in our lives. Rituals take away the sense of the randomness of life. They provide a confidence in the universe that nothing is haphazard or accidental; all things can be categorized under a category. We might not understand why things happen, but rituals place those events into a framework that appeals to our sense of order. They endow meaning to otherwise incomprehensible events and introduce holiness into the world of the mundane.

Rituals cut to the heart of emotion. Rituals acknowledge the part of us that already suspects that textbooks do not have all the answers. In fact, for much of life there is no definable, textbook answer. Rituals are not servants of knowledge in the sense of empiricism but they provide a structure and meaning which speaks to an aspect of the higher self. That is to say, we know that systematic answers to the challenges of the world are needed by the mind, but they do not nourish the soul.

Long, long ago a man was born with everything a parent would like to provide for their child. It was a privileged birth. There was nothing the world held that the boy did not possess. As a child, there were buffoons and companions to entertain him: there were scores of teachers to introduce him to knowledge. As a young adult he proved precocious and energetic absorbing and putting to use everything he had learned. He made small fortunes that proceeded to mount into huge sums. He built massive buildings to house the commodities he monopolized. Soon the man's amassed fortune made him the dominant force in the market. He cut deals and manipulated commerce throughout the hemisphere. People, too, were bought and sold along with craftsmanship. Before long, having conquered his rivals he grew bored, restless. That is when money gave way to pleasure.

Women were trophies to be wooed and won. The man reveled in hedonistic wants and desires. Yet this, too, became tiresome. The game was too easy. The most beautiful women were his with a word. Shaking his head, he immersed himself in wild parties of alcohol and entertainment. All night soirees left him with an aching head and no more sense of fulfillment than before. He pitted his wisdom against the philosophers of the day. He argued, learned and wrestled the problems of the world with them. Sitting and challenging the most learned people of the nation gave him no lasting sense of satisfaction.

It is then that Solomon grew truly wise. His struggle to find the ultimate meaning of life is recorded for posterity in one of the later books of the Bible, Ecclesiastes. Ecclesiastes is King Solomon's testament to the greatest truth he ever found; how to live life fully without being bored, waking each morning with a sense of purpose and fulfillment. The narrative depicted in Ecclesiastes is the question that haunts our days, "Why am I alive? What is my purpose? Surely, there must be more than this!"

Solomon's story reveals most of what falls in our life's experience: chasing the pleasure of knowledge, amassing wealth, pursuing women (or men) is ephemeral. Any such absolute goal gives a boost to the ego before the veneer slips off leaving us naked and empty.

Are we any different? Studies have corroborated what we have suspected for a long time: people work because it gives a quick jolt of satisfaction. Through the bonus, promotion or salutary word, we feel ourselves grow in stature. We then push on to consummate the next deal. As swift as the reward is, the gratification is just as fleeting. Work is not the purpose of life; it is a means. The same can be said for virtually every other human pursuit. Like previous generations, we have mistaken the means for the ends. That which gives us real meaning comes from a different place, as Solomon learned.

An Answer

From the Ancient Zohar: A human is composed of three primary elements: the Soul, the Spirit and Self. The first two -the Soul and Spirit - operate on the plane of the esoteric and ethereal. Soul and Spirit are gifts of God and exist in continual partnership. Each possesses great secrets and understanding that we were never taught, yet whose knowledge resides within us. Significant moments during our lives are punctuated with a wide-eyed awareness when the Soul and Spirit suddenly touch the outer rim of our Self. Suddenly, we are startled by an open awareness of the world when all the mysteries of life are no longer opaque. A crystalline clarity touches all our senses and we are aware of who we are and why we exist. Such moments are so powerful that they leave an imprint on us for the rest of our days. Much of what we know and intuit comes from these treasured gifts, Soul, Spirit and Self.

Just the fact that we *know* the Soul exists, is perplexing. There is no proof for the existence of the Soul, and yet even atheists speak without blinking about a person's soul or complain of a soulless society.

Those first two - the Soul and the Spirit – stand at the highest levels of a person. They are repositories of deep knowledge. The greatest sense of satisfaction emerges from this place. United, they are joined by the third, the Self, in the lower realms (we will learn much more about these three components of our being in chapters 9-12). The Self competes; it yearns for conquest and pleasure; it primps and is vain. Not so dissimilar from Freud's understanding of the ego, the Self is akin to a driving hunger which, when given disproportionate attention, saps or bypasses the positive energy from the other two realms. When that happens, instead of paying attention to the needs of the highest levels of our being, all our energy goes into dwelling on the constant gnawing in the belly. The Self is often mistaken for our entire being. When people dwell on the needs of the Self for a long time they come to forget about the other parts of their being.

The Self is easily mollified and easily challenged. Like a child, the Self deals with surface issues. In an uncomplicated, linear way, all it sees is what exists. The unseen, the spiritual side of our being is not considered as helpful to the needs of the Self. After all, the Soul and Spirit does not focus on competition; they do not vie for accolades and awards. They do not help when waging war. They do not conquer. The Self sulks and demands. It grows needy and diffident. Its needs are addressed by society. The Soul and Spirit meanwhile are motivated by things that society does not reward. This is where our woman cannot understand why her husband just cannot stop trying to solve her problems and instead quietly hug and comfort her.

Consider the meaning of "Thou shalt not covet" in the Ten Commandments. Is the idea of coveting, wanting something that you do not own or have, really so awful? This sin is up there meriting a place next to "Thou shalt not murder" and "Thou shalt not steal" and "Thou shalt not commit adultery." Is coveting really so bad?

The commandment of not coveting is widely misunderstood.

'Covet' itself is not a sin: it may even be one of the better human instincts. It could be argued that if humans did not covet they would never become ingenious and creative. Wanting life to be better is a good thing. Often one of the great motivating forces behind wanting life to be more comfortable, less painful is desiring what we do not have. 'Covet' is good....it is that which emerges from the 'covet' that leads to great inner pain and outer destruction.

The way the Masters understood 'covet' is the relentless pursuit of physical things which are transformed into alternative gods. When the Self is 'let loose' with coveting, terrible things can happen. Knowledge can be made into a god. When we judge people by what school they graduated from, how many honors they achieved or how many big words they know we are no longer looking at people we are genuflecting before the god of knowledge.

Money can also be worshipped as the ultimate goal of life. There are people who respect only those who live in the "right" neighborhoods, drive the "right" cars and send their kids to the "right" school. Anyone else is only tolerated.

The full range of human challenges and avocations can fall into the category of coveting from weight lifting to sex to eating. Coveting is a nagging, deep hunger that cannot be fully satisfied. Once one goal has been achieved - the company has been bought, another degree has been earned, another mile logged - it can only be replaced by another temporal goal. And the hunger is universal and never-ending. It feeds into itself.

In fact, it is much worse than that. The thing that initially provided a wonderful feeling of accomplishment that bordered on euphoria swiftly dissipates until the Self spawns a new purpose; it needs to find a way to exceed the previous goal. A mad repetitive behavior ensues that spans years, sometimes decades. In time though, the façade will fall away leaving us naked and vulnerable. All beings fall prey to the compelling, demanding needs of the Self.

So why do we even tolerate the Self? (Why, indeed, do we even have one? But this is an issue for theologians to argue). Why not abandon it and live solely in the realm of the pure?

A devout Master was deeply discouraged about the prevalence of evil in the world. Evil was far too strong and held humanity in its unrelenting grip. The saintly Master prayed to God to remove the evil force within humanity. And God listened. Because of the Master's pious prayer, the part of us which is evil, the part that possesses an insatiable hunger, was removed from the world.

The Master was happy as the next morning, people all over the world woke to find themselves content. They did not argue, fight or compete. They abandoned war. People were satisfied with what they had. Throughout that next day, there were no buildings constructed, no enterprises begun, no babies conceived. Contentment came with a price: complacency. It was then that the Master understood the truth: the world needs the Self in order to exist. Our task is not to get rid of it but to harness it.

The Self can be the cause of great creativity and strength or invidiousness. Think of a business partner whose fierce competitiveness allows the company to swell and increase profits exponentially. People applaud his business acumen. He receives awards and salary raises for the ingeniousness he brings to the board and stock holders. All this appears as the solid black line at the next Board Meeting.

However, what the black line does not reveal is how many necks were crushed to achieve that goal. On the other side of this black line there is something that crosses over from admiration to loathing. In his unyielding quest for further sales, there lay great swathes of broken bodies. Many people enjoyed success because of his drive. They purchased new homes, were able to buy items for their families, eat and find joy. On the other hand, how many embittered people were hurt by his zealousness? Are there employees who fear and tremble at his presence? Competitors who are now 'on the dole'? Or is it possible that everyone stands in awe of his creative genius?

The Self, in its essence, is not negative energy. Only when it is given unbridled rein over the other two elements does it transform into a dark force. Optimally, all three aspects of the individual - Self, Soul and Spirit - need be drawn upon and used by a whole person. This makes a complete person. However, far too often, this is not the case. In modern Hebrew, asking a person about their well-being translates to, "Are you whole?" Implicit in the question is that when the Self is fragmented, in turmoil and segmented from the Soul and Spirit, the person is not a complete being.

When one of the three elements of a human is compromised, it is usually the Soul. In most people, the urge to preserve and cater to the Self is so powerful that the Self is almost never neglected. Think of all the workaholics whose chief goal is the next sale. They leave early for work, come home late, nuke dinner in the microwave and devour it while watching television. Only in rare characters like Mother Theresa or Gandhi does the Self become subservient or work in tandem with the Soul and Spirit. Few are the saints among us.

To make matters worse society, on the whole, does not reward the uniting of the Soul and Spirit. It only recognizes what it can empirically test; that is, the Self. Little wonder then that our age has produced so few holy men and women while billions are candidates for hypertension.

A question I have frequently asked successive classes of my high school students is for them to name their heroes. When I posed the question, "Who are the people you venerate? Who comes to mind when I say the word "hero?" I have heard many responses. At the beginning, I expected to hear explorers and discoverers, holy men and women, their minister, their parent... What I heard surprised me. The heroes of today they cited were the winners of the "American Idol," television show famous movie stars, and athletes in the football, baseball and soccer world. They named heroes who are not known for contributing anything that made the world a better place. These people were known to have "made it." They were rich, renowned and successful, using all the indicators that these high school students had stressed to them since the day they were first able to talk. These so-called heroes only demonstrated the ability to beat their closest competitors. They smashed the opposition and did a victory dance at the goal line. With role-models like these, is it any surprise that generations of youth do not aspire to change the world? That they are not seeking inroads to their soul?

In fact, the most deeply spiritual of people are spoken of in scornful terms. One of my parishioners was a couple where the wife worked long hours and made lots of money. Rarely did I see her except on special occasions. The husband once confided that his wife would often make derisive remarks about him at home about his religious inclinations. He came to see me deeply pained that his attendance at services was the target of her ridicule.

Those who yearn for holiness are generally viewed as people who need to "get a life." They are viewed as fruitcakes and misguided individuals. "They'll grow up some day," is the usual response to their spiritual pursuit. Anecdotal evidence as a minister has brought me to the painful realization that I heard far more complaints from congregants who bemoan the fact that their offspring are on a religious quest absorbing an Orthodox lifestyle seeking access to their Soul, than those whose children are unethical entrepreneurs.

Yet, most people experience an awakening at some point in their life. Brought on by a death or mid-life crisis they turn inward with their angst. The voice of the Spirit speaks and its sound is most uncomfortable. It tears at the fabric of what we considered inviolate. It asks us what we have been doing with our life. Now, defying all we have stood for, all the beliefs we have harbored, this jarring voice demands to be heard. Joined with the Spirit, the Self takes the person and asks when this awakening occurs: 'Is this all there is?' This is the "ah-ha" moment experienced by Solomon toward the end of his autobiographical Ecclesiastes. It is then that we either dismiss the voice as nonsense or attempt to integrate it into our Self.

א א א א א

There are two negative outcomes to being secure with our Self and wind up feeling like we have failed. 1) We may force ourselves to endure an entropic existence. Many people had this experience when computers were first introduced. The thought of using one of those machines was so daunting that people developed mental blocks against learning that technology. Others experience the same feelings of inadequacy when faced with programming the VCR. The same can be said for any new idea and way of interacting. Or 2) grow bored with the banality of work.

I was sitting in my office during my first week as a newly ordained rabbi. I quickly arranged the two chairs so that they faced the desk. Some thoughtful congregant had the forethought to place my name in burnished letters on the door leading to my office. *Cool*! Waiting for my first customers, I hurried to make the rest of the office appear hospitable. A considerable amount of time went into arranging and rearranging the furniture, placing items on my desk, organizing the shelves. After a few days of hopeful waiting and rearranging, my first case walked in. Sitting down opposite me he told me that he was going to commit suicide. Hmmm. There was not a lot of attention paid to suicidal clients in school so I muttered the first thing that came to my mind.

"How are you going to do it?"

He looked at me as if I just got off a space ship.

"What do you mean, 'How am I going to do it'??? What kind of shit is that? You're not supposed to say that! Here I am telling you I am suicidal and that's all you can do?" "Well, what am I supposed to say?"

"You are supposed to talk me out of it," he explained in an exasperated voice.

"Oh."

I went on to tell him that I, too, had often been frustrated and felt like there was no reason for going on. We spoke from the heart before returning to the subject of how he contemplated killing himself. After a while we were laughing and devising ridiculous methods of ending it all. We left with a hug.

Since that time I have learned the correct responses from the professionals. Their advice was to find out what brought on such a dark wish. Get them into treatment. Bring in a relative. Don't leave them alone. There are many fat tomes written on treating suicidal people. The trouble with all these pat answers is that it leaves out the element of learning, listening and growth. As a novice, I stumbled onto one great truth of life: **Be open**. And since I did not have adequate training to deal with my client I was at an advantage. I dealt with the man in front of me rather than a textbook response.

"Give me a sense of why I am alive. Sometimes it all seems so futile.... Yet the fact that I am here must indicate some purpose for my existence...if so, what is that purpose?"

The disadvantage of knowing all the right textbook answers is that all situations will then appear to relate to or mimic one another. Nothing is novel. Nothing is new. One of the greatest causes of burnout is boredom, where all things begin to merge and blur. The "Been There Done That" mentality reeks of an open yawn. Any position or job has the potential to become banal.

One friend has switched jobs five times in the past ten years! An exceptionally bright and talented woman, she swiftly masters new tasks. Continually in search of the job which will excite and enthuse her, she nervously scans the newspaper for the one position that will save her from the grip of boredom. She can never find it; her relentless hunt can never yield fruit. The hunger comes from within and will never be sated by feeding her Self.

> "Once I was in the deepest of contemplative states," said Bar Yohai. "I saw in a vision a streaming ray of brilliant light of gathered circles. In the center of these circles there was a still, quiet darkness. Inside this still darkness was a single point that loomed brighter and yet deeper like a vast ocean where all the richness of the universe was held. I then asked, 'What does this mean?' And I was answered that it represented forgiveness."
>
> *--Zohar*

In this tale from the Zohar, the mystic, Bar Yohai, had an experience that illuminated his understanding of the force of human-Divine connection. He saw a black pool of wonder that signaled the greatest gift of God and potentially the greatest human achievement, forgiveness. The forgiveness that bar Yohai discovered is not limited to letting go of past hurts that others have left on him. While it certainly involves absolving them of the scars they caused him to carry to that point in his life, it means so much more than that.

A more powerful notion revealed to the holy master was that the path to real growth commences with forgiveness of the Self, which then allows him (bar Yohai) - and us - to move to the next stage of growth. In other words, religious folks tend to speak in terms of forgiving others for their crimes against us. That forgiveness allows us to leapfrog beyond the cords tethering us to past pains that are always present, like a dark shadow trailing us. Those past hurts keep us belted securely to the past, and therefore incapable of being fully present. While this is true, a far more powerful act of forgiveness is to move beyond the crimes others, and we, have committed and focus instead on forgiving others as well as ourselves. In acknowledging our part in the painful experience we then seek forgiveness from God and Self. In that act, we will experience a freedom never imagined. In fact, that moment transforms us into open vessels ready to see things we have not seen, ready to hear words we have been deaf to, prepared for the healing that brings wholeness.

While being open to the world is the first major step in approaching the Kabbalah, it is very difficult to be receptive to novel ideas and experiences if we are still caught in the grip of the greatest internal pain, our sins. While one primary objective to attaining the supernal Light is the realization that nothing physical exists that will satisfy our burning need for meaning and another that a blanket openness is required by us, we will be stymied without the act which lies at the core of all. The point of beginning for this journey, the iridescent pool that lies at the center of our lives, is forgiveness of our Self.

Let's review some of the germane issues here: There is nothing we can hold or attain that will bring us a life of happiness. The physical universe proffers no such panacea. Knowledge too, has a specific use and brings a certain fulfillment but it does not bring contentment. So it is with all things. If we have grown to feel less and less of the vibrancy and zest of life, if we have found ourselves lurching from one new toy to another, it is probably a sign that we are ready to grasp that these ephemeral things are not what our life is about. Almost like a high, the novelties bring momentary relief from the day's drudgery, but then comes the hangover. How do we escape another hangover? Another toy. Then the hangover once more. So goes the cycle. They bring no lasting joy. We are bored.

Boredom is an insidious disease, which affects us all. Boredom undermines our potential: it makes new situations appear like cookie-cutter issues thereby dulling our response to them. There is no joy in the old been-there-done-that. Not only does this attitude make us less effective in whatever we are doing, it also infiltrates into other parts of our life, like a malignancy. It grows, making us feel unhealthy and lacking worth.

The first rule of Kabbalah is to be open and aware that no two situations are exactly alike. We have never been alive in this place, at this time. This moment comes only once, never again. It is therefore holy, laden with possibility.

There is no such thing as a pat formula that will respond to all issues. It does not exist. The now is novel. Each circumstance is unique. Each moment is a new creation. It has never happened before and will never occur again. We all know stories of old businesses that sour and eventually close because they do not allow for change. They are too rigid in their approach and cannot respond to new times and trends. Then there are the other organizations that continually re-invent themselves. They have a better shot at prospering. Why should it be different for us as individuals?

The key to development, growth, and freedom from becoming bored is to view all things as new. Sometimes this means rearranging the furniture in the office, or playing new music; sometimes it entails entering into a dialogue with someone you have seen countless times but have ignored. There is an ancient saying that all people are messengers. They carry words for you. However, if ignored the message goes unheard. Forever. There is no way to recapture either the moment or the message because they are inextricably linked. It can only happen once. The message goes undelivered and we miss the opportunity to change ourselves or the world. The upshot? Go and greet the new universe.

Be aware. It is very tempting to slouch back into old patterns of behavior. It takes a conscious strength to be aware and remain open to the world. Sometimes, it will mean having to repeat to ourselves, "This moment will never recur." It is here once and like a package it needs to be carefully unwrapped and appreciated.

Underlying the whole concept of being fully aware - the response to the question of *why am I alive?* - is that in order to find the answers to the questions which tug at our psyche we must absorb the lesson that forgiveness is bilateral. We need to forgive others so that we can hear the message they carry. As my father, of blessed memory, used to say "Do you think that being angry hurts them? It doesn't matter to them that you are angry." Anger affects only you. Also, how can we grasp the fruits they carry when we cannot see them for who they are? When we only see them in the shadow of the past prejudices that we bear we do not see them at all. At the same time, forgiveness of the Self is critical. It is not possible to approach life with an open eye if we are kept back by the crimes of our past.

That black pool referred to by bar Yohai that lies at the center of our lives is inescapable. Until we have finished our business with the past, obstacles are going to continue to get in the way of moving into our present. That tiny black dot in our subconscious has the power to consume us, undermine the joy of living and sabotage our future. Too much is at stake to simply ignore the center of our being. It is such a vital aspect of growth that it is well worth our time and energy to take some of our allotted minutes of the day and either correct the wrongs we have committed or, if that is not possible, forgive ourselves. Once we have accomplished this task of being open we can approach our present unimpeded.

Sometimes being open and aware means taking time to breathe. Literally. Just stop where you are for a few minutes and listen to the sound of breath entering your body and leaving it time and again. It is a wonderful relaxation tool used by yoga enthusiasts because it is a way of slowing life down. Being aware of the patterns of breathing also makes us appreciate the simplest grounding of life, air. Contrast breathing with our daily lifestyle. They are at extremes of our personhood. That is, they are opposites. Yet, both are integral, necessary for a life that is whole.

Eating is necessary and like all other regular features of our life has rituals associated with it. The rituals of blessing our food makes us slow down and appreciate the source of the food and heightens the mundane event called lunch to a new spiritual level. All this -- being open and aware -- is for the purpose of regaining a vertical connection to the universe. The Self has taken control of our view of the world. We live and operate through our tactile senses, ignoring the sublime. Accessing the Soul then is a kind of reuniting of our true being. It's about becoming whole. And fully alive.

Chapter 3

Caring for the Soul and Self

> As the Holy One fills and sustains the universe, sees and yet is not seen, lives in the innermost place and is utterly pure, so the soul fills and sustains the body, sees and yet is unseen, abides in the innermost place and is utterly pure.
>
> *--Shimi ben Uchba*

Fact: There are ten times as many people on earth today as there were 300 years ago.

Fact: Time magazine reported that in 2000 the European Union grew by 343,000 people. It estimated that India's population grew by that same figure…in *one week* of 2001.

Question: Where am I? With a world that is rapidly filling, why does it seem that my life is becoming less and less important? Is my life of any consequence? Do I matter at all?

It is a shrinking world with billions of people populating the reaches of every conceivable point on the map. This busy planet is becoming so densely packed that it is increasingly difficult to feel like we matter. What difference do we make? Reality shows have come to take the place of a reality life. The population explosion, the crowded highways, impassable sidewalks, blogs and web sites vying for our attention, cell phones, iPods carrying the newest shows and so much more, crowds us. Space has become so limited and confined that sometimes it hard to find where we are in this human mass. It is easy to feel insignificant.

Events domestically, much less globally, seem to be far removed from us. Another war, more deaths in the mid-east, another suicide bomber, threats from rogue regimes throughout the world make us feel overwhelmed. As the news rushes at us on seven different stations, it is impossible to register all that is swirling around us. As an individual do you count at all? Or are you just an insignificant statistic? Kabbalah has a definitive and unique response.

According to the Kabbalah, there are two universes which exist simultaneously. Although our eyes are able to perceive only one of these places, we are told by these ancient mystics that there is far more than that which is seen. Another, higher level of creation exists beyond the scope of our physical senses. Despite the fact that there are two universes, they are bound seamlessly into one whole. The universes are mirror images of each other and, at the same time, are attached. What happens below is reflected above, and vice versa. In religious terms, this means that every action on earth affects the goings on in heaven inasmuch as what happens in heaven redounds upon the earth.

In one ancient, holy prayer, Jewish people utter, "May the One who makes peace in the heights bring peace to us." This expressed hope begs God to allow for peace to flow downward from His universe into ours. The Kabbalistic view has a slightly different dynamic than the one spoken in this prayer: The Kabbalist does not wait for God to bring Creation to wholeness. He acts. Their belief is that we have partnered with God to bring a fractured universe to wholeness.

In every sphere of our life, we have a choice to be active or passive. We can watch events from the sidelines or we can be a part of whatever is taking place. For the religious person, the same is true: we can be involved or be an observer. We seek out the place where we can be best entertained or we can actively seek God. As a mystic; there is no choice, there is only involvement. One cannot be a Kabbalist and remain passive, an observer. To abandon the gift of participation in the world is to malign the gift we have been awarded. To be inactive, in other words, is akin to spitting into the face of the Divine One. As every person's life is of infinite value, action is of paramount importance.

The Kabbalist fully grasps the power of his existence in the universe. It is not beyond his ken to move heaven's hand by his own actions. The mystic knows he can influence the cosmos. Everything he does is of consequence. He knows that there are endless repercussions to all that we do. This construct places humanity in an immensely powerful position. What we do, how we behave and treat each other changes the course of the universe. You do not just matter; you are needed.

Think of it: our seemingly insignificant actions can be the catalyst for harmony- or chaos- for the universe.

From *the Zohar*: Every day a voice calls upon all people in the world, "This depends on you...."

Scientists are just now becoming keenly aware of the interrelationship between all living things. Left by itself, life on earth is in a state of equilibrium. All organisms interact on some level to ensure the continuity of life. Waste products of one organism are used to fuel another. Oxygen converted by plants is indispensable for human life. Even death and the ultimate decay of life is part of the cycle of renewal and stasis. Nature is delicately balanced to ensure that life is renewed. That chain of life consists of interlocking links that forms a great circle. Each life makes possible another's existence. We are linked, connected to all else that is.

Conventional wisdom of the biological variety has it that the frog is nature's equivalent to the miner's canary. Miners traditionally brought with them down into the earth a small caged canary. If the miners accidentally hit a vein of lethal gas, the bird would inhale the toxic fumes and quickly die. That would be an immediate warning for the workers to swiftly exit the mine shaft.

In much the same way the frog is an indicator of global toxicity. It was noted a couple of decades ago that numerous frogs were being born grossly malformed. Some were missing legs, others had too many appendages, some had a single eye.... In certain areas, as many as sixty percent of the frogs were misshapen! Compounding the problem, in 1997 a *New York Times* article told of protozoa that were ravaging the population of certain South American frogs. While the base source of these events in question is not known -- many believe that higher ultraviolet rays or contaminants are to blame -- scientists agree that the decimation of certain species of frogs in the Southern Hemisphere is, in the final analysis, attributable to human interference.

That equilibrium which has maintained the balance of life on earth for so long is in jeopardy. Human contributions to the pollution and using up of natural resources have created an imbalance in nature. Disturbances to the environment have triggered other unanticipated changes. The immediate result is that the most sensitive creatures are being affected by changes initiated by us. Frogs are but a single and early casualty.

When an insect that controls blight in Africa is imported to the United States to perform the same function, it is not surprising when there is a ragged twist to the story. Here is another example:

The same was true of DDT. While this insecticide helped us to manage pests, it had the unintended side-effect when birds also ingested the chemical and, as a result, laid eggs with fragile shells. There have been species of birds threatened to the point of total disappearance from the world as a result of this pesticide.

CFC's, used in refrigeration, were first vigorously tested to find if they were toxic to humans. When the CFC's were found to be relatively harmless it was made widely available to manufacturers and almost universally used. No one then suspected that these inert CFC's would have the unintended consequence of dramatically eating away the ozone layer surrounding the earth.

In 1935 a natural remedy was used to control beetles damaging the sugar cane crop in Australia. A toad. This simple creature was known to dine on beetles with great relish. It was a perfect organic solution. Toads were imported from South America as they were a natural enemy of the cane beetle. No one then suspected that this toad introduced into the region would soon have a devastating effect on the environment. In their original, natural habitat, toads provide an important function in maintaining the equilibrium. But that only works in South America where their natural enemies keep their population from overwhelming nature!

There is a new plague in Queensland, Australia. Scientists are now busy experimenting with viruses to control the toad epidemic. I wonder: Are they considering what unintended effect this new virus might bring?

Everything we do is connected to the universe. All life is a balance, an equilibrium. Any disturbance in the balance will have far-reaching unanticipated effects. A play by John Guare, *Six Degrees of Separation*, portrayed this idea on a human level. All the people of the play find themselves in bizarre situations, entangled in relationships which overlap. Nothing happens in a vacuum. No word can be spoken that does not have an effect somewhere else. At first they just seem like coincidences until all the players criss-cross lives with one another. Everything and everyone is connected.

The play was first brought to my attention by a young man who had just returned from college. Mike played a game with his friends on campus to find a linkage between any randomly named actor and Kevin Bacon. Here is how the game works: one person mentions an actor and the other people's job is to identify, in six stages or less, a correlation with Kevin Bacon. One person would mention John Wayne, and the rest of the people would have to find correlates that wend their way to Kevin Bacon. Perhaps one of Wayne's colleagues had an agent whose son became a movie star. That actor then appeared in a film with Bacon (this is all made up, by the way. I failed miserably playing the game.).

So, too, I came to learned that every human being on the planet can be related to anyone else through a maximum of six cross-relations. We know somebody who knows somebody (add a couple more who-knows-somebody's, if necessary) who knows the Queen of England. In other words, we are connected to everybody, everywhere.

Looking at Mike's game from a different perspective, what happens outside the self also has an impact on our internal life. In other words, just like we can identify or connect with anyone in the world in a few steps, they can also connect with us. This has far-reaching implications. There is nothing which happens in the universe that does not impact on us. If we read a newspaper article about an earthquake in another part of the world, our day is altered because of that information. The knowledge has an impact on us besides any environmental repercussions. The same knowledge shared by billions of people on the planet will also shape the globe. A car beeping its horn at us will also have an immediate effect on us and then beyond us. Perhaps it will put us in a bad frame of mind and be intolerant when we next come into contact with someone. Each event causes a never-ending chain of reaction that can span the globe.

Everything matters. Everything is connected. More, our consciousness is *forever* altered by a new event or piece of information.

Each action, every bit of information that we experience or absorb becomes a part of us. Even if we no longer remember that event any more, it becomes embedded in our sub-consciousness and will thus exert an influence over the rest of our life. The field of psychoanalysis is predicated on events of the past influencing present behavior. Childhood events are recalled to give clues to the present. As one wit put it, "The past isn't gone. It isn't even past!"

Kabbalah expands the idea that all things are connected to incorporate that any change in the world, **known or unknown**, will affect us (and ultimately the cosmos). All things, living and inanimate, are connected. Even a moved rock changes the world. Perhaps a person walking will trip on it, not knowing it is there ("Gee, that's strange it wasn't there this morning."). Maybe the rock camouflaged or protected a hole and an animal is longer safe from predators. Someone or something will be affected by that innocuous move. The ripple effects of that transposition may never be known but it will still have a profound effect of the universe.

Another example. I parked my car at a friend's home during Halloween. Some kids – I assume it was not a rowdy band of senior citizens -- came and let the air out of one of the tires, climbed onto the roof and hood of the car and put dents in it that are still there. From the teenager's perspective, it was harmless fun. They went home and probably do not remember the event even now. For me, it changed my parking habits. I never randomly leave my car anywhere without first thinking what might happen to it. Even more telling, there is a lingering suspicion I hold about roving bands of kids. Everything that happens carries unanticipated and inevitable consequences. Perhaps the Kabbalah version of Mike's game is: No Degrees of Separation.

Just as we understand that the universe is impacted by us, the opposite is true as well. The air we breathe, the houses we build, the songs we buy and the deeds we perform are informed by the universe. The world moves us in unanticipated but palpable ways. We do not live in a vacuum. We are all vulnerable to, and moved by, our surroundings. Some people suffer, for example, from light deprivation during the long winter months. They become saddened, depressed by their environment. Others spend the warm summer months in sealed air-conditioned rooms rarely venturing outside. The loud music coming from next door impacts our mood. It is therefore critical that we attempt to live in harmony with our environment. This means making our inner and outer selves to act in sync with each other. Blending the outside environment with the inner décor creates harmony. How is it possible to control the universe? What can a person do to exert some control over their environment instead of being controlled by it?

Let's turn our attention to one simple way that we can exert control over our parcel of the universe. Here is the tale of one friend: Henry was a condemned man. Henry's life was not too different from incarceration in a prison. He worked in a tiny cubicle inside a massive structure, housing hundreds of employees. For eight long hours each day, Henry had little contact with anyone despite being surrounded by so many other co-workers. Being a bit player in the large corporation, Henry was given his small allotment in the center of a great labyrinth of intermingled rooms only separated by moveable walls. There was no window, no sunshine, and no relationship to the outside world. Just Henry. Nine-to-five in a colorless, flat environment. Looking around at his off-white sterile cell Henry began to feel closed in, confined.

During lunch one day, Henry set off to the local fabric shop and returned an hour later with some blinds and a large picture of Hawaii. Using a few screws, pins and a lot of ingenuity, he constructed a "make-believe" window on one of the bland walls of his office. The blinds were set into a square he marked off. Behind the blinds, Henry placed the poster of Hawaii. Sitting down behind his desk, Henry then gazed out his "window" and looked at the beautiful Hawaiian landscape just outside his office.

Henry grinned and explained, "When I get tired of the sunshine in my "window" I close the shades. I like having my office in the tropics but sometimes the light just gets too bright for me," he told me smiling. "Maybe I should bring sunglasses with me to work tomorrow!"

We are influenced by the space that surrounds us and, as we learned, we have the ability to shape that environment. Our environment can help us focus and be productive or can channel our dark side, our anger. Colors and light alter our attitude in ways we may not be unaware of. In Genesis, "God said 'Let there be light' and there was light." Reading the narrative very carefully, it reveals that no sun was yet in existence. That luminary would not be created for another three days! The sun would not be created until the fourth day! What kind of light can exist without a source?

What was this light that God created, if not light from the sun? That light, according to the Kabbalah, was the light of the inner eye; the kind of light that we perceive, not just what is physically present. Perhaps a more specific word for this perception or vision would be **insight**.

The primal light, the one *before* the great star we call the sun was brought into existence, God calls "good" unlike the later luminaries. God ultimately separated the two kinds of light. The one which is imperceptible to the eye is the inner view, our insight. The other light is for the benefit of our physical sight, sunshine. Of the two sorts of light, the first is the essence of what makes us unique amongst all of God's creations. It was this pure light that enabled primordial man to peer from one end of the universe to the other (we will learn more about this later). This is the true and first light of the world. It is what enables us to *know* things we have never been taught; to intuit ideas we otherwise would have no right or reason to know.

The Kabbalah raises a challenge on the basic question of perception. It states, "The Bible is written with black fire on white fire." To paraphrase, when reading the words before you - right here on this page - are you looking at black letters on white paper? That is the usual way we think about words in books. The Kabbalah challenges this perception though, and asks if perhaps we could conceive of black paper overlaid by another sheet of white spaces so that the words can shine through? Could this page be a black piece of paper, not white? Is it possible that to make the words appear on the page, someone placed over the black page a white overlay with letters cut out making it appear as if the actual page is white?

The Kabbalah asks us to look at the world with a different perspective. Perhaps our preconceptions distort reality. Maybe one of the first steps in gaining a foothold of a manageable life is learning to look at it differently. How we see and interpret the world is determined by the way we look at it.

If you are looking to build a more fast-paced energized workplace, give it splashes of bright colors. The colors will suggest movement, urgency. Vertical stripes further push the envelope toward an environment which encourages productivity. If you need calming down, paint the room with softer hues.

Hospitals are just discovering that the traditional monochrome colors of rooms and walls were depressing. It did nothing to lift the spirits of the patients, their attendants or visitors. Critical to the recovery of patients as well as the attitudes of the doctors and nurses are their surroundings.

Certain colors evoke powers. For example, things clear and blue evoke spirituality and creativity. They are the colors of the Highest spheres. Emerging at the outset of the biblical narrative, these two colors of the firmament are the primal energies of the universe. They are creative, introspective powers. Be aware: as they are primal colors, their power is sheer - they can also be intimidating. So if you plan on redecorating your office, be advised that colors, shapes, positioning of objects will lend themselves toward energy, strength and vitality or the opposite.

Absolute colors like black and white are the tones which show no movement: they are still. These are the colors of nothingness. And they intimate power. They existed before anything recognizable came into being. Black and white swirled throughout the cosmos before the creative processes were ever set in motion. That is why these two colors are barren. Yet having said this, there is a great paradox in black and white. What is black? Is it just the absence of white? People are not even sure whether they are even colors...perhaps they are the absence of them? That is why white and black are not comfortable, settling colors. Like the words were written with black fire on white fire. Unlike other colors, these two cannot be defined; their import is not to be apprehended.

Colors of action like red and yellow comport power and movement. They are anything but static. Fire engines are red because they impress urgency. They are sweeping movement. Red was chosen as the color to arrest our pace. That is why it means 'stop'. It is also the color of blood, and therefore of potential sin. All road signs that want to attract our attention are yellow. It is a cautionary color. It says 'be careful'. It is no accident that red and yellow are also the colors of fire. Colors of change, flux.

Earth tones are the stuff of humanity. They are where we come from. Recorded in the opening passages of the Bible is the description of the first being crafted by God from the ground. In fact, the first being's name was not "Adam." The Bible references him as "*the* adam." What is the difference between "the adam" and "Adam"? In the original Hebrew, the first man's name is not his name at all! "Adam" is a descriptive term meaning earth or dirt. The word 'adam' is thus just an explanation of where the man came from, not his name. It is also our ultimate destiny. Humanity is of earth both in our creation and final return.

The inner ambiance needs to parallel the outer ambiance. The soft colors of the natural world in which we live, the life-giving greens, the earth-toned browns, resonate most deeply and effectively. Yet, shades and slightly variant colors can also make a difference. In this environment, greenery adds acceptance of nature to the room. A plant makes a statement about embracing life, working within the world, not just mastery over it.

The same is true of sounds. Most of what we hear nowadays is white noise. It permeates virtually every sector of our lives. The dull, white noise that indicates the gentle humming and whirring of machines may be conducive to rest, but it does not address the more creative yearnings of the soul. In fact, it is nearly impossible to hear silence at all. I have often wandered deep into the woods throughout my adult life to feel less of the daily hubbub and more peaceful in nature. Yet, I am always amazed that even on mountaintops I can still hear airplanes overhead, horns blaring in the distance.

Oftentimes, soft music soothes and creates a productive environment. Sometimes we need to hear the whistles of the birds calling in the trees. They sing to the soul. Even so-called "dentist music" calms the nerves of the person in the chair with a probe in her mouth. Soft background music can also redirect the uncomfortable pressure when we are standing in proximity of another's aura (think of elevator music and how it relieves the silent anxiety of feeling like you need to do or say something while confined in the small box). What is critical to understand is that various noises, including silence, are needed to nurture the soul. Be attuned to the needs of yourself. Ask yourself, "What sounds are conducive to my produc- tivity?" "What makes me feel comfortable and energized?" "What makes me slothful?" "What do I need to hear to be deeply contem- plative? Or not hear?"

All the feelings of comfort that we experience from being at the shore or walking through a forest arise largely from our sense of the hues of the earth. It also arises from the place of our birth: the earth represents our ancestral start; the ocean reminds us of the mother's protective womb.

Our environment impacts upon the way we approach life. The colors and patterns we use to craft our space influences the way in which we work and play. That environment is a soulful reflection of who we are and, in return, will reflect back to us the attitude and feelings that we want to maintain. This brief excursus into our physical surroundings is meaningful but of far greater impact is the way which we use this attitude towards the balance of our life.

א א א א א

The basic textbook of the Kabbalah is called the "Zohar." Throughout this book passages from the Zohar are quoted that lead us to new approaches and understandings of the cosmos and our self. The word "Zohar" literally means *light*. The Zohar's light provides a shaft of illumination to intensify our perception and experience of the colors, shades and shadows of the world. The way we see things is shaped by *how* we see things.

Were you ever been totally wrong about someone? Were you ever "way off base" in judging someone's character? Sam was one of those people in my life. He was tall. Really tall. When I was first introduced to him, I had to crane my neck just to make eye contact with Sam. When he spoke it sounded to me like an earth tremor. Sam's voice had such a cadence to it that it was intimidating just to hear his normal speaking voice from afar. Coupled with the features of a deeply lined face with none of the tell-tale crow's feet around the eyes which might indicate potential humor or kindly disposition, Sam was an imposing figure. The edges of his mouth turned down. In short, I was frightened of him.

One afternoon, Sam came to me to speak about a problem he was going through. We shook hands and he sat down on the couch in my office. Seated and comfortable, Sam began to speak with his booming bass voice as I attempted to keep my body from sliding under the desk that separated us. I half expected the picture frames on the wall to start shaking. Sam began telling me that he was not a 'regular' at services and that he really did not know me...but needed to speak with me confidentially. He then started to open up his heart to share his pain about his son. "I can't tell how this is tearing me up inside, rabbi...it is so unbearable..." As he spoke, tears leaked down his cheeks and his resonant, tremulous voice shook with anguish. I began to see this man in a new light; his light, not mine.

How we see things, our perception, informs how we interact with the world. After this meeting with Sam, I began to be open to him as he really was, not as I imagined him to be. Isn't it a shame, I began to reflect, that I missed so many other opportunities before this to have meaningful exchanges with him? Whenever I saw this giant of man lumbering down the hall I quickly found something else that desperately needed my attention so that I could avoid him. Who knows what opportunities were lost because of my misperception? *What* we see is colored by *how* we see.

Why do all these things-- the way the universe appears, the interplay of understanding with our inner eye versus our outer vision-- matter? Do they really make any difference to one's life?

The Master wanted to change the universe. He desperately wanted peace. So he prayed for direction from God. The Master looked Above for the message which would launch his journey. Where should he start? If the world was to be re-shaped, how should that change begin? The more he thought and prayed, the more the Master realized that the task would have to have humbler beginnings. It was simply too large a job.

The first objective, he came to realize, was to pray for a change in his country so that they could use their leverage to alter the ways of other countries. So once more, the Master prayed and considered what he must do. Still, to be honest, even this task was far too massive. He then understood that the path to peace would have to begin first with his state.

He came to the conclusion that this was much too large in scope. The Master began to pray that he could start by bringing peace to his city. Still, even this goal was beyond his ability.

Finally, the Master admitted, "Even this is too much. Lord, if I can just have the strength to change my family, perhaps I can then work to change my community."

After yet deeper reflection, the Master said, "This is too much for me. God, give me the power to change me."

The wise man sat down and prayed hard about how be could become more human.

The way up begins with a downward movement. The starting point for changing the world commences with finding and nurturing our internal universe. In taking ownership of our inner world we become effective pilots of our own ship, our self. It is hard to find a niche in the outer universe until we have first mastered the small but critical space in and around us. The ancient ones recognized this when they said that each person radiates an aura of four feet around them. That is why, the sages warned, we must ask permission from the other person before entering into that four foot radius. We are told by these Sages to literally ask someone if we may enter into their space. This is the sacred aura that every person carries with them. It is there when they sit, stand and move.

For the spiritual soul yearning to reach outward to grasp greater meaning, the journey commences at the roots. It begins with where we sit, how we dress, the immediate surroundings in which we are placed. Mastery over our space is like the way we decorate our home.

Now to the crucial and ultimate question. Why is learning about sounds, colors, environment important to the soul? What does it have to do with the soul at all? Even more, what does all this have to do with Kabbalah? The starting point for accessing the soul lies within you. That is why it is so important to be being fully aware of where we are, how we feel, and the triggers of our many emotions.

Kabbalah witnesses the marriage of mind, body and soul. These three areas of a person ought to be inseparable (often they are divided which is why we are reading this book- to find the glue to connect them as once before). The cornerstone of approaching the most meaningful kind of life begins with comfort within the self. Just as one does not start a building without a solid foundation so we do not begin the long journey into the reaches of God and self without adequate preparation. On our journey the primary, the very first, provision that we require is ownership of space. In all houses of worship there are invariably seats that "belong" to old established members. They come every week, having initially found an unoccupied seat and filled that seat for months leading on to years. It became their sacred space.

In my first congregation there was an old gentleman who came early every Friday night. He would arrive at 3-5 minutes before services began and hobbled down the center isle until he came to the same seat he sat in every other Friday evening for as long as anyone could remember. One night a new, potential member meandered into the hall, earlier than Mervin. He looked around and found a good seat for himself, Mervin's.

Not two minutes later Mervin came strolling in (you could almost set your clock to him) and turned to see…what? Mervin stood there like a stone casting an ominous shadow over the newcomer. Slightly to the left of the newcomer, Mervin remained, staring. It looked to me that Mervin was struggling to appear nonchalant but everyone in the congregation was holding their breath, fearful of what might happen. I prayed that Mervin would not fall like an avalanche on this poor unsuspecting soul, who was at this moment thumbing through the prayer book. When the stranger finally looked up, Mervin cleared his voice then smartly indicated, "You're sitting in my seat."

The odd part about the whole story was that this was a moveable sanctuary. All the chairs were fold-ups and the set-up in the sanctuary was literally different every week! It is doubtful that anyone ever had the exact same seat.

The physical space that we create is important. Sometimes the space finds us. We wander through the woods and find a soft place of pine needles and simply sit there feeling the awe and joy of the place. Other times we need to make the space for ourselves. A chair positioned just so in the den or a picture next to the bed might create the right atmosphere for us to feel good. It is a comfort zone. Everyone needs it. What Mervin intuited about holy space is something that is a prerequisite for all people who seek a higher self more proximate to God. One important step in this process is about creating that space and defining it in consonance with our soul.

What we have long suspected about ourselves is true; there is far more to us than we know. We are not simply creatures that take up space, breathe and die. We are woven of fabric that is vast and intricate. The critical task at hand is to attempt to discover who we are and what our potential is. One area where we need to devote time and energy is the space we need for comfort, the colors we use to craft that space and the sounds that make us feel uplifted. Many questions remain. "How far can I run without stopping?" "How do I reach the stage of contentedness?" "Who am I?" Finding the answers to these questions is an individual journey that we have begun. The steps taken along the path of this journey are leading us to the fulfillment of the soul.

Let's review. You are not merely important; your existence is vital to the cosmos. Inasmuch as there are two universes that are reflections of one another, each person is an actor that plays a significant role in this world and beyond. That actor – you -- is irreplaceable. Think of the awesome underlying idea here: Every participant in the drama of life has an irreplaceable role to play. Nothing and no one is redundant. No one is expendable.

We are all interconnected and, as such, are powerful forces for a great and unending chain of change. To advance our potential for positive, meaningful growth and contributions to the world, we need to consider our home, work environment and wherever we are because these have a dramatic impact on our inner world.

Space is important. Each of us has an internal vision of the sacred space we need to create. Discovering that internal vision requires some experimentation and effort on our part. Yet when we create outer space that matches our inward ideal, harmony is achieved.

Remember Henry: We replicate the warmth that begins within. To that extent, we need to take enough time to craft our holy space. It is important to search inside of ourselves to find the place, the color and the position of everything as the Soul directs us. The search for this harmony starts within. The purpose of this exercise is twofold:

1. We need to create a friendly environment where we can sit alone and be comfortable with that simple act and
2. This sets the stage for the reach outward in the next few chapters.

Inasmuch as the place where we spend time must be conducive to the blending of the two great universes, it is ultimately our attitude that informs our surroundings. To be frank, we can find God living in a cave. The similarity between the cave and your living room is that in both instances sacred space must be demarcated by the Soul. It must be created. What we craft in our mind is the most powerful force that we will ever reckon with. We have a great gift of perception that is insistent; it wants to be heard. Our internal light, our insight, desperately tries to reach the surface in us time and again. This voice causes much dis-harmony in the self when we pretend it does not exist. It is the primal light, the fire within that burns inside. This is the point that connects with all things.

Don't forget, the place where heaven and earth connects is you.

Chapter 4

Forgiveness,
the Path of Light and Darkness

I was conducting services aboard a luxury cruise liner. The small community of people aboard the ship was disparate and fascinating. Passengers came from different regions, distant countries and diverse backgrounds. They brought with them stories of famous personalities in their family lines, tragic deaths from which they were recovering, tales of holidays and forecasts of what lay in the future. A disproportionate number were gay. Many were very hungry spiritually for anything proffered. Some seemed to quietly, almost invisibly, slip into the back of the room. I later learned that for many people this was the first time they had been to a service in years. I suspect they felt safer to come to religious services here as there was little risk of being embarrassed so far away from their homes. They were strangers and it was very comforting to know that every fellow traveler here was also a stranger.

I stood near the entrance before the service, shaking hands as people wandered in. Exchanging niceties as they passed, I looked at my watch and decided it was time to start. I went to the front and introduced myself.

"Please take a prayer book on that table," I pointed in the direction of the neatly stacked books.

"Welcome. I am glad you came today. It is my pleasure to be with you today and throughout the voyage. I hope you will let me know if there is any thing I can do to make this service or the trip more enjoyable for you. Now, if you will turn to page three and join with me..."

Just then, a finely-groomed man walked in and interrupted the service. He announced in a voice clearly intended to be heard by everyone, "Hi. Sorry, I am late. Look, how long are services going to be?" He looked at and pointed to the watch on his wrist. "You see, I have to be somewhere in fifteen minutes..."

Waiting a moment, he continued, "Will the service take long?"

"Make yourself comfortable," I answered. "I am not sure how long we are going to be. Whenever you need to leave.... and I am just happy that you are here. Stay as long as you can."

With that exchange, he sat down and we began our service. He stayed and stayed. I peeked at my watch and was surprised he was still here. And then I noticed he began to cry. I realized that his opening announcement, the loud declaration as the service began, was intended to declare his vulnerability. No one could pressure, attack or embarrass him (too much) because he was leaving in a few minutes. By coming to the service he was opening up some deep spiritual or psychological pain that he had unsuccessfully tried to cauterize. In joining the congregation, this man was exposing that wound. That is why he outwardly declared that it was his right to escape, if needed. He was trying to tell me at the beginning this was a dangerous move on his part. He was frightened and needed to know he could leave if what he deeply feared might happen, actually happened.

It was a moment of transposition for me, an awakening. Here was this loud, obnoxious man who disturbed the texture of a calm, meditative service for everyone by his intrusive entry to the room. Now, before my eyes was a needy, wounded man in need to acceptance. It endeared him to me that he summoned up the inner courage to come at all. This was no small thing for him.

His boisterous announcement, "I have to be somewhere in fifteen minutes," was not a warning to me; it was meant as a protection for him. He needed to know that he could run away, if something happened to expose the depth of his woundedness. He felt somewhat safer when he established at the outset, that he could leave any time he wanted. And secondly, whatever burden he was carrying, he was willing to allow that burden an opportunity to heal. In other words, he was willing to forgive whatever past hurt had precluded him from joining community. In a few short minutes, a miracle happened, a man forgave himself.

Forgiveness of oneself is no small thing. Living with regret of things in the past effectively prevents us from living in the present. It is not possible to take in the full measure of joy in the world when the past is not past; regret is like an endless reel that never stops re-playing the same scene. Perhaps the act of not forgiving oneself is a taste of hell. In our mind's eye, we are always looking over our shoulder waiting, expecting something bad to happen. 'It happened before,' we reason, 'it is therefore bound to occur again.' A life of not being forgiven is a life with a close and dank shadow casting its pall over our soul, making the world dimmer, keeps us from being who we need to be. We can not go forward if we live the shadows of yesterday. The feet of the present become mired in re-playing past hurts that make it impossible to move ahead. Such nurturing of past wounds sucks our life-blood, our energy, our ability to be present.

Alvin sat down across from me. "Rabbi, I don't know how I am going to get through this. You really don't know me --I am sorry about that -- but it is for a very good reason. I am terrified about coming out in public and being asked to do anything in front of peo-ple. If I think it is even a *remote* possibility that I will be called upon, I spend the whole night in a sweat, thinking about all the things that are going to go wrong. I will imagine each one of the missteps I will take with great clarity. It's like a nightmare. I see myself making a fool of myself by tripping or saying the wrong words or doing something stupid. Every day, since I was a kid when I was supposed to make a grand entrance on a stage for a school play, and messed up so badly... All I heard was people laughing at me. Everyone was nice afterward, making excuses for me, but I knew they thought I was an idiot. Maybe because of that, I cannot get up in public. Now comes my son's bar mitzvah next month and I do not know what to do. I am terrified and I can't do it!"

I could only imagine while Alvin was speaking, what precipitated his visit to me. I am sure he had long discussions (read drawn-out arguments) with his family about his participation. I was also reasonably certain that Alvin's wife would not be happy about her husband's lack of a involvement in this once-in-a-lifetime event. "What are you afraid of?" I ventured. "What do you think is going to happen?"

"You name it. I have had visions of everything from my zipper being down to my voice cracking. I will mess up the words. I could even pass out! I just can't get up there in front of everybody."

"Alvin, What do you think really *will* happen?"

He began to shift in his chair. Alvin's skin paled and he looked at his shoes. In his face, I saw him thinking, '*He's going to force me to get up there.*' In that moment, I saw a man terribly frightened. Really terrified.

Twisting in his seat even more, he said in a shaky voice, "I don't know but it will be bad. Really bad. I am sure I can't do it."

"Well, you are right," I answered, "You can't do it. So let's think of some way you can participate in the celebration that will bring you joy and not pain." We went on to speak of ways that Alvin could contribute in a meaningful way with his family. From blessing his children before the service to writing words down that would be presented to his son on the day, we brainstormed ideas and possibilities for a long time. I could see this father visibly exhale and relax his taut body as he heard that he was free.

This might sound like an easy way out of a difficult situation on my part but if a person has so convinced himself that he cannot do something, he cannot do it. No amount of reasonable arguments will change their mind. Their mind has already been made up. The decision to not be part of his son's move into manhood was determined long before this man entered my office. If Alvin could have stood at the front of the sanctuary, even a bit unnerved and timid, he would not have come into my office this day. He was desperate and wanted me to tell him that everything would be alright. He would not be called upon and become the laughingstock he knew he would become for the whole community.

Could I have 'forced' him to participate? Probably. I am sure that if I told him he had to do what all fathers do for their children, he would have shown up on that Sabbath morning with great dark bags under his eyes. It would have tortured him through many sleepless nights. Furthermore, I am confident that such a demonstration would not have changed him into a fearless congregant, one capable of mastering his life and fears. The nightmares would continue long after the Bar Mitzvah had ended. Why? He would probably would spend untold hours hyper-analyzing each moment and cursing himself for each movement; even if he was just sitting still. Why put this man through an agony that his mind was not ready to conquer? This tender father was traumatized by the past event and he probably relived the pain of the remembered scene countless times every day and, with each mental reenactment, the old story most likely grew more grotesque.

The inability to escape the prison of the past is all about self acceptance and, even more importantly, self-forgiveness. For Alvin, he could not let go of some unspoken trauma. If he were able to release that pain, imagine what he might be able to accomplish! His past was his present. Like the Sisyphus legend of the man who was damned to roll a rock up a slope for eternity, Alvin suffered from the same complex. He would relive and endure the pain forever. Alvin's past was more real than his son's Bar Mitzvah.

When I was a young, recently ordained minister I would publicly state, and even argue the point with people, that anyone could be an Einstein, Newton, Picasso or Pavarotti. Real genius, I would explain, begins and ends with believing in yourself and not being fettered by the weighty chains of past failures. It is only fear that keeps us from being a creative genius. What keeps us from reaching the heights of which we are capable? Our progress toward the summit is only limited by our fears. Fears of how we will fail, fears of being criticized, fears of inadequacy, fears based upon some past pain, conspire to stop us from becoming the best us.

There may be natural gifts or propensities, inclinations or desires that people have, but it is ultimately faith in oneself that enables us to excel. Imagine the heights we could scale if we had of belief in our own powers! All those dreams that we harbor about what we could have been if only...we had enough time... if only we were given the opportunity as a child... if only we had enough money... the right spouse... a good enough education....

Over the years, I have had many heated discussions with people about the idea that everyone possesses unlimited potential. Most people are either lukewarm to the idea or dismiss it as ridiculous thinking. For those people who took umbrage at my theory, with whom I had this conversation, they felt that my belief was laden with too much guilt. In essence, they told me that I was labeling them a failure because they were not the best in their field or the prodigy their mother told them that they were. No wonder they so adamantly resisted the idea! It is so much easier to blame life than to engage in the healing process of letting go, forgiving oneself and reaching toward wholeness.

Nowadays, when I meet someone who admits failure and **tells** me they cannot do something, I have come to realize there is little remedy for their powerlessness. If they tell me they cannot do something they have effectively closed off that avenue of personal growth. In effect, they have made up their mind. I cannot dissuade them. "You are right," I tell them. "You can't do it."

Envision the great feats we would be capable of achieving if we only had faith in ourselves that we would succeed. Instead of internally arguing for our failures, why we are the way we are, making excuses for our ineptitude, we might actually uncover great reservoirs strength lodged deep inside.

To date, no one has yet cogently convinced me that they know who is eligible for heaven and who is damned to hell. I have not met anyone who has possession of the exact criteria for admittance into either realm. There are a lot of people who claim they have privileged information about who is going where for what, but I am dubious that they really **know** anything. Lots of opinions. Few facts. My point? God alone is the judge.

We have reasonably clear instructions on behaviors that are delineated in the Bible. The holy Book also contains detailed punishments for not following the commandments or for performing a forbidden act. What comes next? The Bible is silent about what follows after the crime. It is understood that a just society need rules of governance. This makes sense. But in a religious world, what follows afterward? We have little guidance here.

If we do not know how God will treat our shortcomings, our sins, then what should we do with our guilt? Beat ourselves up? Flagellate our bodies? What do we do with all our fears based on past experiences? Since we do not know how our sins are going to be judged, what punishments or rewards are awaiting us, what do we do with all our psychic baggage? In religious terms, does it stay there forever? Are we ever absolved?

That mindset of unremitting guilt is simply too unhealthy to live with it. It is toxic to our wellbeing to remain in the depths of anguish. Moreover, it is society's job to govern and God's job to judge. In truth, even in a court of law, the responsibility of the hearing is to restore the aggrieved to wholeness or punish the victimizer but it is not their province to judge the character. That is to say, once a verdict has been issued and the punishments meted out, that is the end of it. The burden should no longer be carried. The weight of a crime forever carried is oppressive and will prevent us from becoming what we are meant to be. Like Sisyphus with his rock; who wants to be eternally cursed with reliving the same sequence of events? Is this what religion and God wants? In a word: No.

There was a joke circulating a few years back. A man receives a telegram which reads: "Start worrying. Details to follow." There is a great truth in this one-liner. The fact is we spend untold time and energy agonizing over things which we have no control over or which have already occurred. That kind of living is at best a waste of our precious life and, at worst, a destructive lifestyle and even the cause of a premature death.

There are specific tasks that we can do to salve our pain, forgiving ourselves for what is in our past. The raw details are found in the Bible in both Numbers and Leviticus and are further developed by Sages throughout long epochs. There are four physical activities to perform when we have done something bad to another person:

1. Say you are sorry.
2. Do something appropriate to make amends for the wrongdoing.
3. Don't do it again.
4. Move on.

Understand this: when a sin has been committed (fill in any noun you would prefer, e.g. crime, affront, attack...) by you or against you, continuing to live in that painful moment impedes spiritual growth. When you are stuck, you are stuck and cannot move forward.

Jonathan M. Case

א א א א א

From the pages of the Kabbalah:

"And God said let there be a firmament in the midst of the waters" Genesis 1:6.

With these words the Holy Scriptures begins to unfold in detail the processes of Creation which began with dividing the waters above from the waters below... This "division" [firmament] brings us to an understanding by which we are able to distinguish between right and left, the right corresponding to light, illumination and harmony while the left leads to darkness, evil, discord....

Moses pondered long in his studies over this section of Genesis. Moses understood that the creative Word appeared in the universe and became the point which was able to join the right and left and then began to weave them harmoniously together and making possible the existence of vegetation and living creatures, all life. Discord and chaos vanished. Peace prevailed.

Moses became aware that the initial conflict between light and darkness was like the present quarrel between Korah and Aaron, the High Priest. After deep contemplative study, Moses thought: 'It is my responsibility to harmonize the discord between Korah and Aaron just as there was reconciliation between light and darkness at the moment of creation: I must make peace between them.' Moses went out but found that Korah was taut, unyielding, not wanting to forgive. With his entire being, Moses tried to arbitrate between the factions and failed. In bitter frustration, he said, 'Korah has rejected counsel and all attempts at dialogue. That intransigence has made a Gehenna [hell] into which he will fall.' In refusing to accept Moses' words of peace, Korah demonstrated that the dispute was not for the sake of truth and God after all. He had no desire to heed the divine example of reconciliation where opposites work harmoniously together. This was the sin of Korah...

First, forgiveness forms the backbone of the universe. It is a Divine principle, articulated by the Kabbalah, that opposites need to work as one. The right side needs the left to survive and vice versa. Think of it this way: There is no "right" without a "left"; there can be no darkness without the existence of light. Light requires darkness. Both must work together. Good cannot exist without evil as a balance in the universe. Korah, a man who was caught in the web of his past, was incapable of extricating himself. Korah could not see the ultimate meaning of using his power in concert with the other side, Aaron. Like light and darkness, Aaron and Korah ought to have worked together to make one cohesive whole. This union was needed by the universe. Instead, Korah chose to work in a vacuum, by himself. As a result, Korah created only evil, a dark cavernous hell.

Second, forgiveness gives backbone to the individual. The act of forgiveness breathes the air of humanity into our being. That is, forgiveness not only mends broken relationships, it also mends the self. It makes us whole. Korah was fearful that forgiveness would damage his persona. In the passage above, Korah suspected that if he was willing to compromise it would be perceived as a sign of weakness. Korah's stature would fall. He would, in the process of making peace, be sacrificing something larger, unnamable; something from which he could never recover. Is this true? When we apologize, are we diminished? Does it hurt us? Is it painful to admit we were wrong? Put differently, do we have to screw up our courage to take the step of saying we are sorry? If so, perhaps this may be a signal that we are like Korah, fashioning our personal hell, because we sense that apologizing will damage our self-esteem.

For Korah, making peace could have saved his life. It might do the same for us. Our longevity, or at least the quality of our life, is dependent upon forgiveness. Unlike Korah, we may not be swallowed up by the earth as a result of being immoveable but our life will surely become more fragmented as we craft our designer Gehenna, a deep dark personal hell. What puts the stamp of humanity on our face and makes us most whole is when the soul likes what our body has done. That is, each of us is made of light and dark, good and evil. Knowing that we house these different elements, we must allow these forces to work together. When both act harmoniously it mimics the cosmos, as the disparate pieces of the person work in tandem.

There is an old Persian tale that tells of a rich man who sent his servant to the marketplace to buy food. Not long afterward, the servant came scurrying back to his employer with a look of sheer terror on his face. Bolting the door after him, the master asked why he was trembling and so pale. The servant replied, "You sent me to buy provisions. When I stood in the center of the market I looked around

and saw him. The Angel of Death! My body froze. I watched him
as he looked up. With his cold, bottomless eyes, he stared at me.
The Angel of Death breathed and I felt my life being exhaled with it.
Unable to move, I looked as he turned to read from the dry cracked
paper in his hands before turning his awful eyes on me again. I
know that he is coming for me! I have to escape. I must run away.
If I flee to the large city of Samarra, I can hide. He will never find
me there. I must leave quickly!"

Later that same afternoon, the master went into town and saw the
Angel of Death in the marketplace. With his dark threatening eyes
he stood clutching same list of names in his lifeless hand. The master approached the Angel of Death and asked, "Why did you frighten
my servant?"

The Angel of Death then turned to the man. In a voice that
sounded like a parched wind coursing through the desert, he answered, "I didn't mean to frighten him. I was surprised to see him.
You see, I have an appointment with him later tonight in Samarra."

There is no need to run. Whatever is inside of us; whatever is a
part of our destiny, will follow. No amount of self-deception will
save us from ourselves. We cannot hide from it. It is part of who we
are and travels wherever we go. To live for today means coming to
terms with who we are. We are human which means we are fallible,
given to wild bloopers, missing the mark, full of shame and, at the
same time, trying to be in full denial of it. Realizing these human
flaws and owning them can be an act of wonderful liberation. It
means we can forgive others because we can forgive ourselves.
Knowing what fallible, prone to error, creatures we are, makes accepting others so much easier. They are as broken as we are!

Running from the place where harmony needs to be constructed
does nothing to help the soul. That unresolved pain will eventually
catch up with us and will hold our soul ransom. We need to embrace
what we are. We must embrace all the wonders, distasteful or hateful
aspects of ourselves that are a part of our constituency. There simply
is no place to hide from ourselves. What we do not want to own will
eventually find us. We are an amazing blend of contradictions. We
are black and white, bad and good, kind and ruthless, guilty and innocent, Korah and Aaron and so much more. With all these disparate
characteristics we are truly remarkable and gifted beings.

Let's review.

Once we have acknowledged our evil deeds we can move on to a new and higher stage of growth, making amends. It is not an easy task to confront our recurrent nightmares but when we have steeled ourselves for the event; when we are ready to meet the demons that have afflicted us, we will finally have arrived at the place of accepting and confronting who we really are. Only then do we have the option to make it good; turn the evil into good.

One night long ago in my life, the dark memory returned. The memory was never far from my conscious mind. It came back to me bidden, or against my will. This time I was trying to bring it back and my unforgiving memory obliged. Here it was: When I was nine or ten years old I used to visit the local variety store on the way home from school. I would stop there every day with some change in my pocket- a nickel, a dime or even a quarter!- to buy a pack of baseball cards or, if money was short, the flying saucer candy that had tiny, sweet, colored candies inside.

The shop owners knew me well and always said hello to me. I was a school mate of their son. One day on my trek home from school and I came into the store and chose some of the sweets from the front glass case near the entrance to the store. Reaching into my pocket, I did not even have the seven cents the candy cost. Mr. Keytz looked at me, shrugged, and said, "It's okay, Jonathan, bring me the money tomorrow."

There was no tomorrow for the payment.

Soon that forgetfulness turned into a feeling of embarrassment and I just pretended that it never happened. Whenever I ventured into the store, I would secretly pray that they had forgotten my trespass.

Twenty years later, I still remembered my deception and theft. The memory still stalked and shamed me. I told a confidante about the pain and she suggested that I think about it and not to be so dismissive.

"What do you think you should do?" she asked me. "Leave it alone and let it continue to haunt you for the rest of your life? You know it is not going away. Too much time has already passed for that. What *should you do* with this memory?"

Later that same evening I called information and located my old school mate's telephone number. There was not much to speak about. I tried reminiscing but we were not such close friends and finding things of interest to talk after all this time was awkward. So many years had passed since we last spoke. In the conversation, I asked about his parents and how they were doing. He told me that his parents had sold the store years before and both had since died.

Now I was really stuck. I had no one to apologize to! So, I opened up my heart and told him my tale. "You know, your parents were such good people. They always greeted me warmly when I came into the store. And they were always there smiling! Your dad always asked how I was. Both worked very hard. I loved going into that candy store. Even now, I smile when I think about all baseball cards I bought there coming home after school.

I continued, "And I want you to know that they were very good to me. I remember when once I entered the shop and they gave me candy when I had no money to pay for it. I never repaid that money and they were such good souls that they never reminded of it."

"Yeah," he said. "That is the way they were with everybody. Nobody was ever chased out or yelled at. I guess that must be part of their Holocaust experience. They were survivors of the camps, you know. They never forgot what happened to them or their family. I think that is why they were so good. They knew what it meant to be hurt and abused and they never wanted anyone to feel what they went through. They were forgiving and kind."

The moral? Even death does not prevent us from confronting the past.

Forgive.

Don't do it again.

Move on.

Chapter 5

A Reason to Be On Fire

"The candle of God is the Soul of Man." --*Psalms*
"Look at the fire rising from a burning coal…the flame cannot rise until it is tied to something physical." --*Zohar*
"Blessed is the match that is consumed…" --*Hannah Senesh*

"How do I find it? How can I locate the fire inside? I want it to be part of my being. I want that gnawing emptiness inside to become filled…"

Rick, a perplexed and angry father, came to talk to me about his son. He took some lurching steps forward, stopped and appeared to fall down into the chair with a thump! His arms hung limply down the side of the seat, like they had just been deflated. He sighed, "I don't know where to begin. I am so embarrassed at being here," stammered Rick, "and telling you this…Nothing I do seems to ever be enough. I am tired. Sam, my son, is stubborn, obnoxious and hateful. I never thought I would say this about my own flesh and blood."

He stared at the floor. Rick was in deep anguish about his son, a young adolescent going on thirteen. Describing some of the scenes at home, Rick wrung his hands together in a twisting movement that declared he was at end of his tether. Conditions had become so intolerable that there was almost always screaming and, a few times, the situation almost came to blows.

"I never know what's coming next," Rick told me. "Dinner time is full of tension. I don't want to come to the table. I try keeping the television on while we eat to deflect Sam's aggression. All he ever does is pick on the other kids, his brother and sister, and make insulting remarks to everybody."

I asked Rick to name the things he had tried to do in order to change Sam's behavior. "He loves playing his computer games and can easily spend hours at a stretch in front of the monitor. So, I went out and bought Sam's son a brand new computer for his room. I thought it would be great to encourage him to use the internet and develop those skills. I was also praying that he would stay in his room and there would peace in the house. Wouldn't that be great? No warfare. No arguments. Win-win for everybody. Even if Sam were quiet for just a few hours, I would take it."

Rick went on to tell me how amazed he was that now the boy had a computer of his own in his room, he barely used it! Instead, he spent his time terrorizing the rest of the younger children and playing with the family computer in the den.

Remarkable.

I asked Rick if he could make sense of this behavior. Putting up his hands, Rick said flatly, "Nothing works with Sam. I don't know what to do for him anymore. I give up!"

"Maybe Sam is begging for attention," I responded. "*Things* are not what the boy wants. You are great parents. He has virtually anything he wants. Sam is looking for something else."

"Like what?"

It seemed to me that Sam was doing his best to become the center of attention, or at least to be involved and fully accepted as a member of the family. Rick's son wanted to be where there were voices around him and where he would be part of a larger community, even if that meant standing on the periphery and taking pot shots at everyone. Even negative attention is attention. That is why Sam balked at being holed up in his room to play games on his brand new computer to his heart's delight. It was too unbearably lonely there.

Dilbert was a popular new comic strip to hit the market. Its attraction lay in the utter stupidity of disconnected people. Dilbert's world is a universe of dunces, living in a carved-up universe of tiny cubicles, who invariably make bad decisions. Dilbert works for a huge corporation (which I imagine could be a paradigm for a nation, a community or a family). That corporation fosters single-minded functioning with little understanding of the whole. The employees are people who have been forgotten by the world and who have likewise, forgotten it. Their day consists of white-washed walls with no sense of anything outside the daily grind. It is a world of people who have lost the facility of language, connection and teamwork. Like a modern day Babel, people speak but their words are meaningless.

One of the most disheartening things about the computer age is that it physically separates people. Techno-heads escape human contact in favor of surfing the web. On the internet, so many human foibles can be overlooked because they are not viewed through the computer terminal. We are invisible.

And yet. Chat sites are the hottest commodity at homes and offices. In their tiny workspace cubicles, real world Dilberts send out messages to a universe of other Dilberts seated at their desks yearning to make contact with someone. The universal blossoming of the personal "blog" site is another natural sequence to our being so disconnected. Someone can set up their own 'blog' and share all kinds of information about them. On the blog you can read what they like to do, the things they hate; you can even learn their most intimate secrets. Messages sent out into cyber-space allows bloggers to feel that someone out there cares about them, reads about them, takes an interest in their thoughts and activities, even if they never meet. People send messages out with electronic clicks and beeps in the hope of making a soul-ful connection *that is heard* by another human being…even if they are in China!

One of the great successes of our day is YouTube, the ultimate world connection. YouTube spans the globe connecting one person to a limitless audience. This web-site, YouTube, allows anyone with a computer and the ability to record, to broadcast to the world. We deeply yearn for some kind of human contact. While home-computing could easily isolate people in their universe, it has instead fostered a massive outreach to touch and be touched. We want someone to take notice of us; we need to be a part of a community.

Do you exercise? Lots of people do nowadays. Companies in the fitness business are reaping great profits. Gyms are sprouting up like coffee houses and haute couture for the gym rat is now de rigueur. Remember the old tube socks and yellow faded undershirt? Those days are gone. Nobody would dare wear *those* to the gym. Racks and racks of pricey clothes, designed for looking smart while working up a sweat, fill stores.

A professional trainer confided to me, "You don't need all this." He spread out his arm in a gesture to take in all the weights and machines. "Nobody does. Look at these expensive machines. Do you have any idea how much they cost?" He pointed at the array of equipment; weights, Stairmasters, barbells, and the rest. "You can do all this at home with a fraction of this equipment and expense."

I reflected upon his words. If that is true, why are all these people sweating it out in their brand-name shorts and designer tights when they could dramatically cut their costs and traveling time by working out at home? Maybe my friend is the keeper of the world's best secret. Are the exercise barons are trying to keep their monopoly on these fitness centers by not letting anyone know they can do this much cheaper at home? Not likely. Even if they did tell people, I doubt they would listen.

People do not want to work out alone even if they could save wads of money. They look to others for inspiration and companionship while doing leg lifts. Even if they never speak a word to anyone! Passively running on a treadmill, next to someone doing the same, is better than running alone. Any place where people can gather at what used to be the watering hole in earlier times is a glaring human need. Loneliness is the ultimate fear.

That is why records are set and broken in races. People do not usually set records when competing against themselves. Competition brings out the best in us. The ferocity to engage the next-in-line and beat him, is a powerful force. We need other people to thrive and perhaps even to survive. In fact, all life - perhaps with the exception of single cells that auto divide- requires other life to nurture and be nurtured; to validate the existence of one another.

There is good, healthy companionship and there are relationships which cause pain. There are even invisible relationships; the kind which exist in the world of fantasy where relationships are constructed in the mind. All of these; even what we perceive as difficult and even destructive relationships, sustains life and maintains us.

Viktor Frankl wrote one of the most powerful books of our era, <u>Man's</u> <u>Search</u> <u>for</u> <u>Meaning</u>. It is one of the most engaging and life-changing books I have read. Frankl was a survivor of the most brutal of times, the Holocaust. Under constant physical torture, wracked by emotional pain while being robbed of their humanity, few found the ability to continue to live.

Frankl places the question before the reader, how any survival was possible where every attempt was made to dehumanize the victims of the Holocaust. Names were taken away from the victims soon after their arrival at the Camps. In its place, numbers were scored into their forearms. Each victim had only a number now. They were nameless and faceless in the striped rags. Arriving at the Concentration Camp they were bodily shaved and then dressed in identical, ill-fitting, random-sized outfits. The Nazis were adept at shearing every scrap of humanity away from their victims. The Concentration Camps were not only efficient factories of death but the ultimate attempt to degrade humans into creatures less than animals.

How could anyone remain human where all vestiges of humanity were cruelly and mercilessly abused?? How can a person survive when riven of all hope? The brutality of the Nazis was matched by their ongoing treatment of Jews as certainly less-than-human (they were called sub-humans) and less-than-animal. How did those who were able to survive find both the will to live and the ability to maintain an image of their own humanity in the midst of such depravity? This is the question posed by survivor Frankl.

Those who were able to focus on small acts of courage and keep mental images of hope had the best chance for survival. Frankl tells simple tales of heroism like sharing a crust of bread or aiding the sick – even in a vain gesture where the rasp if death was already present - in the midst of a hell that only promised brutal punishment for any acts of goodness. There small acts kept the victims alive. What preserves our humanity is the very act of sharing it. Frankl later wrote that "everything can be taken from a man but one thing: the last of the human freedoms -- to choose one's attitude in any given set of circumstances, to choose one's own way."

In this human made hell, words of hope provided a glimpse of a possible future; they were the life sustaining force of the damned. "The prisoner who had lost faith in the future - his future - was doomed." According to Frankl, survival depended on one necessary ingredient: "A man who let himself decline because he could not see any future goal found himself occupied with retrospective thoughts." For Frankl, the ever-present idea that he would one day be reunited with his wife was the sustaining thought that kept him alive in the Camps. He had a reason to live, something to survive for.

Frankl told of meeting a fellow prisoner in a Concentration Camp who came to him with a dream. This man dreamed that the war would end and they would be liberated on March 13, 1945. He dreamed that day would be auspicious. It was more real to him than the open sores on his body. He knew he would live until that moment because salvation was on the way. It was almost here. The dream was a vision of something to come, a reason to continue to live and look forward to, a future.

When the date finally came, the poor man died of typhus. When his dream was not fulfilled, there was nothing left to live for. March 13 was the ultimate date of his liberation. Quoting Nietzsche, Frankl wrote, "He who has a why to live can bear with almost any how."

Relationships form the backbone of the human psyche. They fill a yawning space inside us that cannot bear to be empty and go on living. Any attempt to forge meaningful relationships with others for our own sake --and giving others the same opportunity -- creates a reason to live. Frankl would never see his wife or family again. Yet, the belief that he would reunite with them kept him alive throughout his journey through the Holocaust. The same is true for the daily bloggers who are also reaching out for a connection, along with the treadmill joggers at the fitness center.

Like the survivors of the Rwandan genocide, the Armenian massacres, Pol Pot, and so many other horrific events of the past and present, survivors were able to cite the vision of a life and relationships that once existed and that they would eventually recapture. That was enough to keep many alive when the awful pain of living became excruciating. Simply the idea that they would re-connect with the stream of human life once more, galvanized their survival skills giving them great internal strength.

People, who have lost the vision of something to connect with, have lost the will to live. Progress has provided the means to not have to rely upon anyone for survival, including our immediate family. We can separate from our family, our tribe, even our nation and still survive. This could not be done in former times. For protection, food, shelter and much more we used to need to rely on a network of others just to survive. Distance no longer matters for many business relationships. The ability to move swiftly and relatively painlessly (think of our forebears who trekked across the prairies to get to the west) has allowed extended and nuclear families to spread out across the globe.

There must be a reason we do not divide our cells like an amoeba in the processes of generating life. We need another. Perhaps this is the real meaning behind God's declaration in Genesis, "It is not good for man to be alone." The Bible is telling us that even if we possess the greatest survival skills in the world, we still need companionship. With people, it takes two to reproduce. We need others in order to reach our potential. Otherwise, we are lost.

Frank Sinatra sang a wonderful ballad by Rogers and Hart called "I Wish I Were in Love Again." In it, Sinatra sang of long nights, brutal arguments, kiss-and-make ups, kisses and hurled plates sent flying across a room, screams and cries of betrayal. It is a tragic and revealing song. Here is one line:

"The furtive sigh,
The blackened eye.
The words, "I love you 'til the day I die"
The self-deception that believes the lie.
I wish I were in love again."

Any kind of companionship serves a purpose that assuages loneliness and providing us with an incentive to live. By the way, this statement should not be seen as an endorsement for staying in a hurtful relationship. There are people who remain in abusive relationships because they are too frightened to get out of them. I cannot help but wonder if the primary reason for staying in such a relationship is because they are afraid no one else could possibly love them. Likewise, there are employees who stay in jobs even though they are being mistreated. I also wonder if they, too, fear no one else would ever want them as an employee. My advice? There are lots of employers out there looking for dependable workers and many lonely people hungry for a connection.

Rick's lonely boy, Sam, cried out for attention. He desperately wanted someone to peer over his shoulder, to give him the quiet comfort of knowing that he was an integral and accepted part of his family even if his angry actions belied that. It is essential to love and be needed. Connection is all Sam required. It is what we all need to thrive and, sometimes, just to survive.

Long before the Scopes trial began, the question of whether the biblical narrative was true had been a raging argument among scholars, atheists and religious folk. Is the Creation story really how it all happened? How can it be that the whole process took a mere six days? What about the dinosaurs? How do they figure into the story? Was there an Adam and Eve who lived in Paradise? To all of these questions I can only answer that I don't know. I wasn't there.

But the tale of Creation points to a more important and profound, lasting truth. After the first human being was placed in the Garden of Eden, he experienced a terrible overwhelming loneliness. The man cried and shivered throughout that long night. He howled at his own helplessness to feel any value at being alive. He needed someone to hold; to give and gain comfort. There was no one. The animals came to the Being (the ancient ones said that the animals of Garden could converse with him.) but it did nothing to lift the blank gray sorrow that hung over him. The man was not happy until he had another like him, Havvah (Eve).

"This is the bone of my bones, flesh of my flesh," he declared. In other words, 'Here's something that is just like me. Now life has become whole and meaningful.' Until this point the Bible is only about theology. It is really just the story of God. The first chapters of Genesis have no existential bearing other than to place God as the Primal Force, Creator of All. Now, as we reach the climax of the story, we find Adam and Havvah and how they discover the basic underpinning of all life, a connection to one another.

Did you ever notice that sometimes the best, most productive workers are ones who live alone? Spinsters who devote themselves to an organization and thrive in their old age? Bachelors or widows who throw themselves selflessly into their work? Their devotion to work is all-consuming. They live and breathe the stuff. The people that they work with and for become their surrogate family and their measure of their selfhood. People need each other.

Janet was one of those people. She was a congregant that was unselfishly devoted to her mother. A teacher by profession, Janet's ultimate devotion was to the woman she lived with. Janet was an 'only' child and so took her responsibility to her mother seriously. She would rush home from school, make sure mom was safe, prepare dinner for them, share the day's events together and end up resting before bedtime listening to old recordings. That was her routine for nearly fifty years! When her mother finally died, Janet was devastated. She had no husband. There were no children. No one. Frankly, I was concerned that she would give up, become sick and die herself (Janet was then in her seventies).

A few weeks afterward, during one of our many conversations, I asked how she was doing. Janet was excited. "Well, funny you should ask. I have a new life. I have become the district tutor for the hard-to-manage kids. These are the kids that can't be handled by the regular school system. They cannot make it. So, I go to their houses every day and sit with them in familiar territory. Most of them are very poor. But when I get there I lift their spirits and teach them all the basics! I love it!"

People do not become what they are capable of becoming, without others. Other people allow us to reach the zenith of our ability. They give us a reason to get up in the morning and live. What every computer geek, every aspiring Dilbert, every hungry kid who hangs out his biography on the web for others to see, every would-be Michael Jackson who belts out a song on YouTube has come to realize is that they need connection. They, like the rest of us, need to relate to others.

Let's review what we have learned. People need people to survive. From Adam to Frankl to 'blogs' the message of connection is expressed by the actions of the living. We cannot exist without others. Computers may be a cover for the pain or a groping mechanism to find a connection but they are only the latest technological vehicle to send a message out that we pray will be heard. To not acknowledge this fact in the great marketplace of life is to miss the evidence that people provide through their actions. Fighting against this trend or proscribing interpersonal contact runs against the human grain. It makes us miserable, unfulfilled people. Companions, friends and colleagues bring out the best in us. They help us to become the best we can be. Even while societal advancements seem to run contrary to this elemental human need, people will invariably seek out others to compete against and to gain praise from them. Might as well capitalize on it in our search for wholeness. When we finally internalize the truth of needing companionship to live, we can consciously devote ourselves to responding to that desire for ourselves.

People provide us with a reason to exist even in the deepest bowels of pain. With no one to live for, we simply stop living. I once made the claim in front of an assembly of doctors (and challenged them to debate me) that more people die of loneliness than any other disease. No one disagreed.

The National Institute of Health found that people who pray or attend worship services at least once per week were 40% less likely to have high blood pressure than those who did not. Other studies have indicated that patients will often say that their religious connection was critical in overcoming with their pain.

Putting aside the possibility of God's intervention, a religious connection does two things: 1) it gets us involved with others. People visit and pray with us. Patients are aware and comforted, even if they are not visited, that someone is praying for their wellbeing. 2) Religious faith is connection with the Other. Even if not a single person comes to visit the infirmed, faith that there is greater love in the universe can stave off the awful silence of being alone. There has been much written on the theology of suffering. Belief in a Higher Being implies that you are never alone.

A Sage approached a Mystic with a personal problem. He said, "I have studied all the Ancient Texts in search of an idea. I have coursed through tomes, heavy with knowledge culled from the centuries. I have studied with the greatest and most learned masters of our time. Tell me, what will make me feel closer to God? Do you have any suggestions?"

The Mystic replied, "You think I am impressed by you and your learning? Your books mean nothing to me. Go out into the streets and meet your people. Feel their fear. Understand what causes them pain. Take the risk of getting involved in other people's lives and then we'll see what kind of a Sage you are!"

And the Sage began to weep.

And the fire began to take hold.

Chapter 6

The Angry Client (at times known as the brooding neighbor, perennially upset relative, human roadblock, a noxious person...a.k.a. your nemesis.)

> **How is it that a tiny candle can shine at midday?**
>
> *-Zohar*

Every place that we have so far studied, the underside of every rock we have turned over and examined and the travels we have made in this book have been prudent, but an underlying question still demands an answer: *How can I achieve wholeness in a world where I do not even know where I am? I am lost. Please help me find me and then, I am sure, I can find my way....* There are many important ideas covered in the first five chapters of **Journey to the Soul**. It is now time to turn our attention to these vexing issues and answer them.

We begin with the inward attitude that people bring to wherever they find themselves. This is important.

For example: Did you ever enter a room and find yourself unexplainably affected by someone else? Perhaps there was a brooding figure in the corner sending out beams of despair. Have you felt those mournful waves? You may have gone in contented and all of a sudden, a feeling of unease pervades your sensibilities. For no apparent reason everyone else also feels ill at-ease. There is a cause for the discomfort, though. It has a source that is emanating from one person in the crowd. At other times, anger so permeates space that it can turn an entire party into a roomful of soft whispers. Such the negative energy can be felt and feels so real that it could be "cut by a knife."

Another example: One person becomes the center of the room without seemingly doing anything that would make them a locus of such attention. There is a kind of magnetism that draws people's attention towards them. Everybody wants to get near them. Our eyes flick in that direction. Such a feeling is almost palpable.

For example: Have you ever been a room where there is an unbridled joy that seems to have its origin in one person? Goodwill and love become so apparent that the very walls seem to want to dance. A place where happiness so permeates everyone that we do not even consider the thought of leaving? We hope the moment will never end? It may not make any kind of empiric sense to say that we can feel something so intangible, but like anger, joy is real as it is universally felt. Attitude creates environment.

How does it happen that conversations can be guided or dominated by a single entity, the same person time and again? How does it occur that a room's essence can be altered by the introduction or exit of one person? Often movies portray a beautiful woman entering a room and all heads pivot toward her to gawk and stare. Or it might happen in another film when a gunslinger stealthily walks into a saloon, a noisy environment is transformed into a wake. Every person carries an aura with them. The same is true of us. The baggage, or idiosyncratic ways of thinking about ourselves, that which we carry with us, creates a power of its own that people instinctively perceive. So how is it possible for us to become a magnet of attraction to others instead of feeling like an empty vessel taking up space? Can we change our aura? Can we become what we are not? Or perhaps, can we become what we know we really are deep down inside?

Inasmuch as a woman's fantasy may harbor the vision of her being the object of a roomful of attention; while a man might covet the gunman's inspired fear, both figures are projections of something far deeper than outward beauty or a cowboy's gait. Have you ever seen a person dress with immaculate, focused precision and yet find their appearance 'off'? Somehow lacking? If we were to carefully examine them we might not find even a single hair out of place and yet there seems to be a pervasive negativity, wrongness or maybe nothing that is remarkable or noticeable about them. Have you ever waded deep into a mass of people at a party and felt almost invisible even when dressed and coiffed to rival a star? That unspoken draw or magnetism, or the cloak of invisibility, has less to do with appearance than something far deeper. The Hollywood lie is that a person's mystique arises from their physical appearance. It does not. Let's look deeper.

The great Sage Joshua was, according to reports during his lifetime -- some two millennia ago -- a very ugly man. One day as he observed a prodigious scholar coming toward him, Joshua greeted the man with warm words, "May you know great peace."

The scholar stopped and stared transfixed at the homely Joshua. He gazed unblinking. Then he blurted out, "How can it be that you are so ugly?"

Joshua responded, "I do not know. But it is the Master who must be asked why he created such a flawed vessel."

The scholar was stunned when he realized his insensitivity. Overwhelmed with shame, he wondered how he could have been so unfeeling and thoughtless. Feeling the choking bile of self-pity, the scholar felt himself going under in a wave of humiliation. He had embarrassed another, a sin according to the Tradition that is proximate to murder. Instead of looking at the Sage and perceiving his true inner beauty, his open soul and generous spirit, the scholar focused on something totally wrong, the container. Joshua's body may not have been attractive but he was universally recognized as one of the kindest and wisest men of his generation.

Although we may choose to occasionally forget that real *power* comes from within, we know it is true. That indefinable reach that radiates out of a person is the place of their authority. Attitude, approach, something almost indefinable, is the real seat of power. Outward appearances lie. Our strength -- what people see when they look at us -- is an indefinable draw that starts from a fire within and that translates itself into a natural energy, or aura, that surrounds us.

Each person carries with them an aura; a kind of invisible cloak that everyone knows is there, but cannot see. The aura is like a mood. It may not have distinctive, visible signs but it is still present. Did you ever meet someone for the first time and take an immediate dislike to him or her? It is not unknown or peculiar to have such a negative reaction, is it? Ever ask why? Chances are the reason you may have an instant aversion to them is that they are having a bad day (there are many other possibilities). Usually our instincts are correct. This probably is not a good time to approach them for a favor or to expect a reasonable response from them. Isn't it amazing that we can sense something negative in someone we have never met before? That is the aura. We feel it, even from a distance.

Auras can also take the form of positive energy. There are some people who carry with them such strength that they appear like an impregnable tower of energy, brimming with possibility to us. Everything about them seems to pulsate with power. We may say of them that they possess charisma. In stature, they may be diminutive, but their aura is one that radiates great power.

This aura can be harnessed and shared. That is why charismatic people have a following. It also explains how cult leaders acquire their clique of supporters. The aura can even take on exponential strength.

The feelings/baggage/aura that we bring with us creates its own picture of who we are to passersby. What about the adage, "clothes make the man?" Can't we disguise what we feel and put on a good show of what we want to project? No, it does not work. As another adage goes, "Put a monkey in a business suit and what do you have? A monkey in a business suit." Just because he wears a three-piece suit, it does not make the monkey a businessman. The three piece suit may do nothing for us too if what is under it does not carry the aura of responsibility and confidence. In a multitude of unspoken and indefinable ways, we bear self-definition. People perceive it. They feel what we radiate and they will be drawn towards us or even repulsed by what they sense. There are also auras which are blanketed under so many protective layers so that these people become invisible; tasteless, flavorless and odorless souls. There are some people who are passed over; they are not seen.

The most critical question for us is: Do we approve of how we are being appraised? That is to say, do we like the aura we are projecting? Is this what we want? If, in our core self, we feel inadequate, that is what we will outwardly project. If we feel empowered, we will radiate that persona. Whatever we think of ourselves will become the aura that others see when they turn their attention to us.

There are times when we are determined to change our aura. We make a start and find ourselves being pushed back into old ways. Sometimes the people that love us the most are invested in making sure that we do not change. That does not mean they do not love us or want us to become better people. It is just not easy to watch someone we care about change. When someone we love changes their behavior or even something less definable like a change of attitude, we become scared. We cannot help but wonder if they will still love us afterward. Unconsciously, they try to force us back to be the old familiar us. They are most comfortable with the way we used to be, the person that is known to them. A change might signal danger to the relationship, they instinctively think.

Teenagers complain that their parents treat them like "babies." There is some truth to this. Parents desperately want their children to grow up and be independent while, at the same time, fearing to trust their offspring to make the right decisions. One certain outgrowth of that maturation is that the children will grow more distant in their emotions until the point when they physically separate from their parents. The prospect of that separation can be frightening. Relinquishing control over teenagers is a risk in many ways. The parents may watch them strive for excellence or witness them make dreadful decisions with long-lasting consequences.

Is this true for you? Do you fear that the more you try to change your modalities of behavior, the more people push you back into "their" expected picture of who they think you are? Is changing outer behavior and the inner aura like swimming against a riptide?

If we are continually treated the same way (and act in accord with the way we are treated) we risk never growing. At the same time, a more insidious consequence of remaining the same is that we are in danger of cementing the image, or mask, that has been projected onto us. If we do not wish to be beholden to the image that others see in us; if we desire to avoid becoming what others make of us; can we change our persona to search out what we really want to be? Must we conform to the way we are seen? The way people treat us? Or, can we find the courage to act in harmony with our self?

You are not going to like the next sentence but it is true: *If you do not like how people are responding to you there is little you can do to change that.* It would be like telling people not to watch a certain movie but giving no cogent reason for not seeing it. Of course they are going to watch it!

We control no one, except the one that stands at the center of the aura; you. The only real power you possess is what lies within you. Then, the way which people respond to what they feel when they see you will, no doubt, be altered as their perception of what they see in you will be different. The process of change is not easy and do not expect people to accept it without a fight. But –and this is important -- the starting point is not changing people's perception of you; that is a red herring. It is the wrongheaded. People will not change because you want them to. Believing someone will change to accommodate anyone else is nonsense. There is only sure way to change the way others see us and that is to change ourselves. Inner change cannot hang on the way we are seen or treated.

Kabbalah is about starting at the beginning of the path. The beginning of the path is the core self, the place where the inner fire burns. Once that core self has been released and allowed to be in synchronicity with our real self, it will inevitably follow that people will react to our authentic aura. Others may well interpret what we then carry as charisma, depth of care, sainthood, confidence, power.... all those descriptions are also not relevant. What matters is to be true to oneself. That is the ground of life.

Idea: The internal fire is fed and nourished when we are true to our self, our aura. From deep inside, the flames that reach upward to empower and invigorate us. When we are in harmony with the voice of our soul, true joy begins to well up from our innermost parts.

We inhabit a universe of the seen and invisible. We are trained and geared to deal with the visible and, on the other side, equally unprepared to deal with the non-physical universe. Yet, that which we cannot physically see is just as real! The client sitting with his arms folded can be felt by the whole office as he steams with anger in his chair. There are no discernable beams of rage that can be calibrated, yet they are nonetheless felt by everyone.

In much the same way, the underlying concept of Kabbalah is that we must be attuned to the invisible. The unspoken, unnamable parts of our lives are often more important than what we have set as life goals. For example, it may be more critical to our life to be serene than rich. Serenity is not a course in college. It is not a profession. Serenity is nothing that can be scientifically measured. Yet, it is more crucial to a good life than amassing a fortune. Throughout our lives serenity is a notion that has never been taught as an ideal... while it has been inculcated in us to strive for wealth and power over others. Serenity, contentment and joy are noble life goals. They feed the internal fire.

Idea: The unseen inner goals we establish for ourselves are vital for our wellbeing. Those goals are personal and individual. We know what is good for us. We do not learn it from television or radio. It does not come from the books we read. What society or friends tell us to seek may not be the path of our inner voice. Insight about our soul comes only from the soul itself.

Idea: We have become so used to responding to what we think people want us to be that after many years of practiced imitation of that image, it sticks to us. The mask of deception adheres to us like a mask that we have long forgotten about. In fact after years of use, that mask becomes our face; it is what Goffman called <u>The Presentation of Self</u>. The professional artist adopts an aloof, fiercely independent posture. The financier becomes the power broker that must instill an all-knowing mask to reassure her clients, the lawyer becomes the pugilist-table-pounding advocate to intimidate the adversary, a salesman adopts a mask of a confidante and on and on. As students of Jungian psychology learn, these masks become so well-used that after time they replace the real us. The mask tenaciously adheres to our outer presentation until one day, unnoticed we have lost our self. *We* are simply no longer there. Only the mask remains.

"How is it that a tiny candle can shine at midday?" the holy mystic wonders.

After all, a candle's light should go unnoticed during the daylight hours. The sun's brilliance would fade any flame into insignificance, especially a minute wick. Yet the candle (like the soul) glows also giving off heat waves which can both be seen and felt. We can see rolls of heat rise from the candle's wick even as the flame itself may evade our vision eclipsed by the sun. We can also feel the heat of the fire as we come close to it. Listen: we may not see the flame during the day, but we can feel it. It is there. Just because our eyes are not able to see it does not mean that it does not exist...

Kabbalah places before us a choice: we can opt to live in the world of deceit, or the world of truth. We know the flame is there because we can see or feel its presence. On the other hand, we could come to the decision that the flame is not really there because we cannot see it. In much the same way, we can live in a world where we say, *only what we see is real.* Or we can acknowledge the world of the seen and the world of the unseen. Both worlds exist says the Kabbalah. We know that fire can burn in the daytime and not be seen, only felt. We choose how we perceive the world. Both worlds are full of the same people- the same bodies, same lives. One can even transition from one world to another without even realizing it. An illustration:

A young student named Joshua -- this is, by the way, the same Joshua mentioned in the passage above -- approached his master with a request. "When will the Messiah finally come?" he begged.

"He is down by the gate of the Old City now."

Joshua excitedly inquired, "Now? He is there now? Where is he? Where can I find him? How will I recognize him?"

The knowing one answered, "The Messiah is easily to find and recognize. You will know him because he is dressed in rags. His body is covered with sores. The Messiah therefore is swathed in bandages which he removes carefully, one at a time. Look for him and you will find him."

The acolyte ran to the place and anxiously looked about for the one. Immediately Joshua spotted the old man by the Old City gates carefully taking his bandages off one by one and then replacing them. Gingerly, the novice Joshua asked, "Are you the One?"

"I am," said the filthy, old man without looking up.

"When will you reveal yourself? When will you come?"

"Today."

Running back to the House of Learning, young Joshua could

barely conceal his throbbing heart and exultation. He prayed throughout the long day waiting for the moment when the shofar- the great ram's horn- would announce the Messiah's arrival. The day passed. The sun finally set and the student returned to his master, not understanding why he was deceived.

"He said he would come 'today'," began the aged master. "What the Messiah meant was that he will come at any moment when the world will be ready to receive him. You see, the Messiah was referring to the holy Writ which states, "*Today*, if you are prepared to hear..." That is why he only bandages himself one wound at a time. He will be ready whenever he is called. The moment when he will reveal himself to humanity is when we are truly prepared to hear the message he bears. He cannot reveal himself if people will not embrace him. What is the point of king with no subjects? Of a Messiah with no following? He would be rejected as an imposter, a charlatan. So he patiently waits down by the path to the Old City keeping a watchful eye on us all. Only when we are prepared, will he reveal himself without hesitation."

The overt interpretation: Humanity needs to be aware that the promise is ready to be fulfilled. We have not been deceived or misled. Deliverance will come. It is almost here. Yet, are we so utterly dependent upon God, so powerless to effect change? No, the story asserts that we have a distinct mission in the universe. The messiah waits to be unleashed. The keys to his liberation lie in our hands. The cosmos needs us as much as we rely upon it. When our words coincide with our actions and when every human being will embrace the holy Word of God, the Messiah will be released.

The Kabbalistic interpretation: Be unconcerned with the goal. There is no timetable for enlightenment or redemption. We may inhabit the holiest of spheres right now and yet be unaware of it. Our life may be predicated on a single moment and if we are otherwise occupied we might miss the opportunity. Instead of constructing sandcastles on the shore, we need to be aware of the power that inheres inside of us. The **moment** may be at hand when the Messiah proclaims is poised to reveal himself. Just as he waits for his moment and must not be preoccupied with his bandages when the time arrives, so too, we must be ready to assume our role.

Preparedness for the ultimate moment in our life means that we wear no mask. We are attuned to the words of our soul, the fire ablaze inside. That mean we are alive, now. The alternative is to be blind to the nuances of life. The many layers of insulation we are wearing will prevent real light from penetrating the mask. We will be unaware of the moment because we are not our true selves.

The idea of anger is a great paradigm for the wearing of a mask. What is the meaning of anger? Anger comes when we are challenged and feel our ego, or mask, threatened. If, for example, someone calls us "stupid" how does that affect us? If we feel endangered because that person has unmasked our true self (that is, we really believe that we might be stupid) bile will rise in our throat; anger and resentment will bubble to the top. Anger most often comes when we feel genuinely threatened.

We cannot stop someone from being hostile or mean spirited but it is within our grasp to understand the how and why of our reaction to it. If we are called "stupid" and feel like an *Einstein*, it is likely that we will react to their comment with a benign smile. 'Ridiculous! I wonder what their problem is', we might think. Our ego is unaffected by what they called us. Strengthen the way we feel about ourselves, the mask becomes looser and our anger level subsides.

Knowing who we are and being in contact with the true nature of our soul is a source of great strength. A person's anger might be the hub of a room's focus but that hostility does not have to turn us into something that we do not want to become: We can hear what others have to say without allowing their words to affect the way we see the world. In other words, we do not have to take on the cloak of their rage; we do not have to become transformed by them unless we choose to have 'bought into it'. We can be attuned and empathic to their mental state of being but do not need to be molded or bonded into their schema. We are not blind to their pain -- on the contrary, we see it very well-- we just refuse to be enmeshed by it. It belongs to them, not us.

Anger is just one form of power that seeks to exert control. Differing emotions are just as potentially real and influential to us. Joy, exuberance, thoughtfulness, calm, awe, are all components in harnessing power when -- and this is important-- we fully own it. Owning our emotions is always a choice. No one foists their emotions upon us; we choose to absorb them. Likewise, charisma is nothing more than respecting one's own soul voice. When we heed our inner voice and act in harmony with it, people say we have 'charisma'. Those that observe us; those who take their behavioral cues from others are doing what we used to do, living their own shadow instead of embracing their *own* true self. It is the midday candle that still gives off heat and provides light. The potential inheres in us.

We all have relatives *and you know exactly who I mean.* Some are full of love and caring; others are full of venom and destructiveness. How to best deal with them? The same way we approach the nasty salesperson or client who can barely conceal their scorn for their job. We do not have to become the person that we used to be. We do not have to accept the emotional scorecard they present to us. It belongs to them. How we feel, how we react is always a choice.

Most things that we are taught in school, at the playground and water-cooler, by our parents and friends is to focus on the world of goals, which in Kabbalah is called the World of Deceit. We are told that if we follow the standard lines of life; education, a large house, bank accounts and the like we will achieve happiness. Generally, we come to question this illusion and scrutinize it later in life. Going through a mid-life crisis is when we first seriously question our pursuits, how we have spent our precious years devoted to the goals fostered by societal norms.

What we discover as we cross this bridge into maturity is that life is made up of moments, not goals and acquisitions. The first stage of our life was misleading and illusory. Our needs could never be fully satisfied by getting 'more.' Fewer people however, manage to get to the next level of figuring out how to translate that realization into a reality.

In the world of Kabbalistic thought, there is an apt illustration of the power of a moment. "Gilgul" is a revolutionary concept, literally. Gilgul means that lives sometimes need to be re-lived in order to complete a specific mission. Our days can be too short to complete our given mission or perhaps a person may have so erred that a return to earthly life becomes necessary. In the universe where we lived before birth, we may have been assigned the task - or taking it upon ourselves as an act of tikkun (repair-work) - of giving direction to another soul, allowing it to reach its zenith. In other words, the raison d'etre of our life may be a single moment, doing a favor, providing a direction for someone. It is daunting to realize that our life may be fulfilled in a single moment....or it may be lost.

Jonathan M. Case

All his life he wanted to undertake the journey. He dreamed of the holy pilgrimage that he would one day undertake. The object? To visit with the holy Master, the Baal Shem Tov. Every part of his being yearned for the opportunity to worship in the presence of his holy light. To be a part of the blessing of his entourage was something that David had desired for years.

Finally, the time had come. David packed his bags and began the long trek to the home of the Master in Mezhibozh. The road was long but spurred on by the vision of what lay ahead, his mind moved across the terrain to the house of the Baal Shem even though he was many miles away. The day he had chosen to arrive was the Day of Atonement. It would be a holy, awesome day. The trip was planned out so meticulously that he would arrive at the table of the Master in time for the candles to be blazing and the congregation swathed in white in anticipation of meeting the Maker.

So many things went wrong with the trip. It seemed that at every turn, David was waylaid by the horses needing new shoes, the wagon requiring repairs....Closer now than ever, David saw that he was only an hour from Mezhibozh. He pushed harder now as the sun was getting close to the edge of the horizon. "I am almost there," he panted as he pushed even faster.

From the side of the road, a man emerged, "Please stop, kind brother."

"Please make it quick," David answered. "Look to the sky. The sun is ready to set. It is very late the Day of Atonement is almost here. Please hurry! What do you want?"

"A favor. There are only nine of us in this village and without an additional soul we will not have a quorum. Would you stay here for this next day? If you remain here, we could pray as a full community. You know the tradition, we need ten men. Without you we cannot say certain prayers..... Our congregation is much too small.... but if you were to remain with us we could pray as a full congregation."

David shook his head. He thought, I have been planning this trip for my whole life. "I am on my way to visit with the holy Master of Mezhibozh. I cannot help you."

"Please," begged the stranger.

But David had already pushed the horses ahead. Leaving the stranger behind, David moved on to Mezhibozh. Arriving barely before dusk, David quickly washed and eagerly put on his white garments, taking his place near the holy lamp. Later that evening, all the students stood in front of the Master and were each blessed by the Baal Shem Tov. Patiently waiting their turn, they bowed their heads as the Master placed his hands on their heads and uttered words of fire and love. Somehow, the Baal Shem missed David.

After the Day was over, everyone present was again blessed for goodness from Above. Not David.

"Master," pushed David through the throngs of students and well-wishers. "What about me? Where is my blessing?"

The eyes of the Baal Shem then gazed at David. He looked startled. "What are you doing here, David? I did not see you. You are not supposed to be here. You are supposed to be in that other town. They needed you for the quorum. You were the one they were waiting for. This is not your place. It was only for that moment were you created…."

Since we are not privy to the moment of actualization, Kabbalah mandates being awake and aware at all times. Our perceived adversary may be the focus of our life's task. Alternatively, we might be theirs. Consider the following:

How would history have been different with a role model directing the young life of Pol Pot?

How many of the walking wounded would be whole if some adult figure had heard their early cries?

How many crises could we have averted if someone just listened to our anger rather than rejecting it? What about the relationships we have ruined because of our rage?

"Loss of temper is disrespect for the Divine Presence," said Rabbah Bar Huna two thousand years ago. Every person, carved from God's image, comes bearing a great truth. We are all much larger, more grand than we have been taught.

א א א א א

So, what then do we do with all these emotions that we feel? What do we do with the angry client, the nasty cousin? How do we deal with offensive clerk? How can we avoid becoming snared into *his* darkness? On the other side, how can we find the holiness that some people seem to so easily grasp? How can we "catch" what they have?

Everyone is a messenger. Each person carries something important for us. After all, if we are unique and gifted...mustn't that also be true for them? As they come bearing their unique gift, we are presented with a choice: We can choose to receive the gift, unwrap the box they have brought to us and accept it or we can refuse to take notice of it. *At all costs, we must not become them - the bearer of the gift - because then the message will be of no use to us. We must not become anyone else; that would be a betrayal of our unique identity and destiny.* Think: they bear a message for us to hear but they do not know the value of the gift that they carry. If they understood the message they could not bear it. The receiver alone understands the true value of the message and if aware, can ferret out the gold from the dross. We alone can decipher the meaning.

When was the last time you received an e-mail with the message appended to the end, 'please send this to ten more people?' The initiator of that e mail sent it out in the hope that the message reaches the right person. Who knows who that might be? They intuit that all that needs to happen is for this message to be repeated with such frequency throughout the world that chances are that it will reach the right eyes. It will wind up in front of the person who can make something of its message that will ultimately impact the world. That is the principle behind the messages that we receive and need to pass on and those that we originate and hand out. Eventually, it will reach the person for whom it was intended.

If everyone is a messenger, we had better be attentive to what others bring to us and not dismiss it. We may be the terminal for the message or we might just be the conduit to its ultimate destination. Anger, indignation and love all have their place too. They reach deeply into the psyche and require hearing. Note once more: we do not have to become the message, just bear it. That is, another's anger does not belong to us; we need only be attentive to what lies behind it.

In one ancient commentary on the Bible, a scholar named Shmuel asks why God continually tries His people with pain. There are times when we even call God angry, vengeful, wrathful, and accusatory. If

God is good, how can He be so full of these polar emotions?

Shmuel goes on to observe that God can be appeased by our contrition. All we have to do is show remorse, do repentance and God smiles.

Is this really possible? Can the Perfect One be so petulant and so easily mollified? No, says the teacher. What passes for anger is a movement to change, a trial that requires a response from us so that a change can occur. In other words, all packages leave some import behind for us, even if we are not looking for them; sometimes, *especially* if we are not looking for them or do not want them. In the latter instance, this is often how we define pain: when things happen to us that we did not plan or want.

Note: In the instance of God's anger, He does not require our becoming angry for Him. The One simply wants a reaction.

Isn't that same true of others? What is needed is that we listen, understand -not necessarily become - and assimilate that information.

Each person carries a message. Every life event and person is a teacher. We must be an attentive and deliberate student; otherwise we run the risk of missing an integral irreplaceable tile in the mosaic of our lives. Yet, if we make the mistake of taking on *their* identity, our journey has been lost and must be regained at all costs.

So, what then do we do with an angry client, the bitter relative? Listen. Do not attempt to wear his cloak. This part is critical and it is where most of us get lost. *It is his coat.* Do not take it from him. It is healthy to empathize with others but that does not mean that we are required to absorb what they carry. Hear the words and listen for the hidden nuance meant just for your ears.

Listen. Repeat. Get it right.

Chapter 7

The Point Where Heaven and Earth Converge

> Then Adam repented.
> Then the Holy One, blessed be He, made for them clothes.
> Only with the indication that Adam and Havvah repented came the abundant light. That is why the Holy Writ goes on to tell us that God made clothes for the man and woman. Only when we realize that we are truly naked, that objects of the universe are mere illusions, are we capable of wearing the cloak of light as our garment.
>
> *-- Zohar*

For Kabbalah there is the obvious meaning of a biblical text and then there is another one around a curve, just out of sight. We are going to peer around that corner to examine some of the hidden elements of Creation. Using techniques of the ancient mystics, watch as the narrative is straightened and then deciphered to yield first its revealed, and then its hidden meaning. Where we begin is at the beginning. We start with a familiar text of the Bible that tells of the root of humankind.

Remember, Genesis opens up with the formation of the universe.

There are no introductions or clues to what came before. Genesis begins without preamble. The drama of the birth of the universe is swift; it all happens in the space of a few unembellished verses. Then the Holy Text reveals the paragon of the creation process; beings cast in the image of the Divine. Placed in the Garden of Eden, the Holy Text states of this new creation, "They knew they were naked." Genesis 3

In order to understand this verse, we must get rid of some preconceptions. 'Nakedness' for the Kabbalist does not refer to not having physical clothes. The two primal beings, Adam and Havvah (also called Eve), understood in their realized nakedness, that all things of this world are temporal. Physical things appear as if they are real and will endure through all time but they are short-lived. That is the meaning of the phrase, "they knew they were naked." They understood that everything which exists - even in the most magnificent place on earth, Eden - is a fleeting gift. The desire to find Atlantis, Shangri-La, Eden or win the multi-million dollar lottery is generally thought to be the key to ultimate happiness. That is the lie which Adam and Havvah were created knowing. Living in the Garden, consuming the fruit of ultimate truth and life, they understood that they possessed nothing; they knew and accepted their nakedness. "They were unashamed" of their nakedness indicates that they accepted their life.

'Humanity,' whispers Kabbalah in the margins of the text 'ought to be full of shame.' Look at our daily pursuits. Examine the clothes we wear to impress others. The way we work inhuman hours to gain a nod from our employers; the way we pretend we are something that we are not; are all markers of the self-deception of life.

A woman died. Sent to the place of Ultimate Justice, the woman stood waiting for the verdict. Judged on the Balance of Life as not overwhelmingly good or evil, the woman was given a choice by the great Ministering Angel.

The Angel extends an offer to the woman, "Heaven or hell?"

"I do not know what choice I am making," she said. "May I see them both before making my decision?" the woman asks.

It is agreed. Whisked off to the nether-world of hell she sees people eating, walking, working, conversing, going about an everlasting existence. "Not quite what I expected," she thinks to herself. Then brought to heaven, the woman sees people eating, walking, working, conversing, going about an everlasting life.

"I don't get it," she says. "It's the same in both places. They eat, talk, and carry on. They look the identical to me! What difference does my choice make?"

"Don't be deceived," replied the Angel. "You think heaven and hell are like the Michelangelo's paintings of Paradise or Dante's vision of Hell. You think that if there are angel choirs, cherubim distributing baskets of love, banquet tables set with delicacies and rich rewards beyond reckoning – it looks like heaven. If there is brimstone and sulfur, screams of pain, wicked punishments and endless suffering, it must be hell. It does not work that way. You are under a misconception.

"The people you saw are not in heaven or hell. Heaven and hell are not places. You see, when a person dies, it is not where they are go; it is what already exists inside themselves. For some, everlasting life is hellish beyond words. They are so unbearably full of bile, regret, anger and lost love that they are forever in a personally constructed hell. In other words, life is hell. For others, sitting in the shadow of God is the greatest blessing. The joy they feel at having lived a good life, a life of doing their best, doling out acts of kindness, yearning for the Heavenly Father constructs an ideal place in the highest heaven. Either way, these people are not in heaven or hell, heaven or hell is in them."

This is the meaning of being naked. Adam and Havvah were aware of their true self; they were at once unmasked and unashamed.

Knowing one's own nakedness in the imperfect universe where we travel is the key to ultimate freedom. Being naked is to see oneself and the world for what it is without deceit. Even in Eden, lush fruits ripen and then rot: trees blossom and then lose their foliage. Life dies and becomes renewed. Nothing is permanent. The eyes of Adam and Havvah were opened to the world. Their eyes, according to the mystic tradition, beheld all of creation. That is, they saw from one end of the earth to the other. They perceived no deception. They witnessed no untruth. Not taken in by the possibility of weight loss, permanent life free from disease or faster cars, Adam and Havvah were simply naked in the world.

What the serpent offered to them was a different kind of vision. He proffered not just a fruit but the possibility of seeing competition, exercising one's prowess against one another, becoming and having more. In short, the serpent promised knowledge of the world that Adam and Havvah did not possess. Wanting to trade the eternal for the ephemeral, the first humans lusted for the fruit. They took the offering and, in the exchange, forfeited Eden.

Why was one of the first actions taken by God to make clothes for the Man and Woman? After all the marvelous creations that the Holy One orchestrated; the emergence of light, earth, constellations, life; why does God condescend to do something so ordinary, so mundane as to make clothes? Is this what the Master of the universe does?

God felt humanity's new-found pain. Man and Woman were experiencing something no other being had ever felt; shame. They understood they were naked before this but now they felt shame at their nakedness. God empathized with their internal angst.

What had changed? Why did they just now feel shame? A powerful transformation had come over Adam and Havvah once they chose to eat the fruit of the forbidden tree. At the moment they tasted the fruit, humanity discovered lies and deceit. The vision of Adam and Havvah before the fruit was unimpeded. They saw and accepted the world for what it was, beautiful and temporal. Now, their eyes saw beyond the borders of the Garden and they lusted for it. Man and Woman were no longer content to see from one end of the earth to the other, now they wanted to conquer it. Part of that conquest meant dominion, having power. Adam and Havvah were now part of the stream of fierce competitiveness of life; now they understood the value of the self pitted against one another. Adam and Havvah were no longer comfortable with their Self. Humanity wanted to hide their true nature. They had breached the walls of Eden. That is when the Holy One decided to make them coverings.

These primal beings were reborn with a sense of competitiveness, self-doubt and shame. Adam considered his physique and was concerned that he was not strong enough. Havvah wondered why Adam looked at her in *that* way. Both vied for control of one another. A great desire and existential fear arose and took hold of the two people. Never again would they or their descendents rest satisfied with their soul without great effort.

What was God's remedy to their shame? God did not just make

them coverings to hide behind. The Holy One made *two* sets of clothes for the Man and Woman. The first set was sewn from a fabric. This clothing covered their different-ness. It was a mask for their bodies; a protection of their vulnerability and shame. Placing the clothes over their bodies, Man and Woman felt a sense of relief from their awkwardness.

The second set of clothes was not a shield to protect them from violent forces and primitive urges. This other set was entirely different; it was a reminder of what Adam and Havvah once possessed. It was a "cloak of light" which they could don and feel the embrace of the holy once again. It would give them a taste of their beginnings in the Garden. When they put on their robes, Man and Woman would feel at one with each other, whole with the universe and one with God. But here is the key: Adam and Havvah, along with their eternal progeny, had to be conscious enough to find the "cloak of light" and then put it on. This is no easy task because unlike the first set of clothes, this one is not physical. It exists in the far reaches of the mind. Only by accessing the higher self, can we find the cloak. We must first search for the garments. Essentially, we are all in search of Eden and the cloak that God made for us to connect with the Infinite and live for a while without our feelings of inadequacy.

What was the purpose of this "cloak of light?" What exactly did it enable Adam and Havvah to see? According to this age-old tradition, the "cloak of light" allowed them to see the universe as it was originally designed and intended, whole and vast. Whenever they and their descendents would choose to wear the cloak they would recapture the expanse of the earth as it reached toward, and connected with, heaven.

Some religions place great emphasis on this world. They underline the importance of the eye's sight, 'the scope of our vision is what God wishes us to be involved with,' they would say. Our world is the *only* world and we must therefore be consumed with only this. There are many righteous acts we are given and told to perform; all of them relate to the here-and-now.

Other religions downplay the world's importance. It is deception and illusion, they argue. Those of mystic faiths tend to minimize the trappings of the physical universe as distractions from what is real.

'Real,' for those mystic folks, is unreachable except by great leaps of devout faith, sublime love and acts of fervor.

Kabbalah holds a different perspective. It tells us to peer behind the curtain: We need to question. If this world holds little or no importance, why did God create it? That would be an act of idiocy and certainly runs head-on into the idea of an Omniscient Being. That God created a universe implies that there was a purpose for that creation. The fact that the One created both this universe and physical beings to populate it (us) indicates that it is vitally important.

On the other hand, if this world were all-important, does that not negate the concept of God and any unseen existence beyond our tactile senses? Put another way, if there is a God then there must be more than what we see. Why would God be limited to what our minds can apprehend? Of course, empiricists are now vigorously shaking their heads. "No! No! They would determinedly argue. The truth lies in between... Science is god". I will not attempt to debate them here; it is not the purpose of this book. Most of us though, are caught in a psychic vise which squeezes our sensibilities from those two opposing directions, the seen and the unseen. For those who *know* there is a God, the question must arise 'what does God mean for humanity?' Or to put it differently, what is the place of God in my personal life?

Kabbalah's answer is significantly different from both approaches: The expanse of the universe can not be quantified. There is no measure to God's power. In one of the most potent statements of theology made in the Bible, it says: "Listen Israel, the Lord is our God, Lord is one." This statement means that not only is the Master of the Universe one but the universe with its Maker is one. Everything that exists, heaven and earth, is woven together into a single tapestry. This is to say that these two universes that coexist; one which we call earth, the other heaven are actually enmeshed to form a single entity that appears separate and disparate. This is an illusion. It is all one fabric. The first universe is the one which engages our physical senses. All that we feel- olfactory, tactile, audibly - is a part of this universe. Everything that we know and, for some, all that exists, is this place. The sciences, that which can be tested, are rooted in the ground of the physical. Connected- and this is a key word- to this universe is a meta-physical universe.

Occupying a conspicuous place above my desk is a picture that has inspired me for decades. It is a simple framed poster of two mountain-tops, one reflecting the other, in Jerusalem. The Jerusalem in the fore-ground is the physical reality of the land of Israel. Atop the Temple mount burns an eternal fire, a vigil pointing heavenward. The other image is a heavenly Jerusalem, a reflected likeness of the first. Im-plicit in the picture is that both Jerusalems are interdependent. They necessarily co-exist. If something happens to one, the same happens to the other. If one fire goes out, the other is extinguished. If one burns brilliantly, the other mirrors the leaping flames. The Hebrew phrase that captures the essence of the work translates as, "If you tend the fires of Zion, so will I tend its heavenly fires."

Heaven and earth are inextricably linked. When there is chaos below there is chaos above. As peace reigns in one realm so it does in the other.

To revisit an earlier question; What is most real, the physical or meta-physical? Heaven or earth? Which do we choose to accentu-ate? The Kabbalist's answer is that both are integral, inseparable. As they are interconnected, what happens in one realm finds its cor-ollary in the other. In fact, David, the Psalmist, notices that "The One who makes peace in the heavens, makes peace on earth." There is no separation, except perhaps in the mind.

A person may choose to live in only one of the worlds but that does not dismiss the other into non-existence.

How does this idea of the connection of two universes impact the living? What does it mean to say that heaven and earth simultane-ously exist and are dependent upon one another? What does this mean for you? This is a critical issue: Everything we do is of conse-quence. If the cosmos is one, if there are two universes that are actu-ally one whole universe then nothing is unimportant or insignificant. Everything matters. Every action taken impacts the cosmos. If heaven and earth are interconnected, where do they touch? You.

Let's review: Just as the holiest of texts contains varied levels of meanings, so does our life. For the driver, the road is smooth and manageable. For an engineer, the road rises and falls and curves at angles that allow for drainage and control at the speed limits. For aesthetics, wildflowers grow in the median showing the awesome power of nature and making the journey pleasant. It is the same road but appears differently to each person. People will attach different meanings according to their varied personalities and mindsets.

On its most elemental level, Genesis provides a framework for understanding human origins. It tells how we were cast into being. It is the story of Creation. On another level, Genesis gives us a glimpse of the vastness of the universe. Even shorn of our raw understanding of the cosmos, God has given us the tools-- a cloak allowing us to recapture that expansive vision of the world. We are human beings molded in the image of the Infinite with infinite possibility.

We are instructed that Adam and Havvah had a great vision of the universe until they wanted more. They desired the fierce competitiveness of life outside the gates of Eden. They wanted to compete and conquer. They surrendered the gift. When Adam and Havvah relinquished their hold on Eden, the two beings lost their vision but gained a new, different kind of sight. Yet, in their diminished state, God left the keys in their hands to reclaim the far sighted understanding of the cosmos, a second set of garments made from supernal light.

On yet an even higher level, the tale indicates that heaven and earth are connected. Humanity once straddled both universes. Now, we are born into one and, with effort, gain glimpses of the other. Our feet are connected to the earth while our head rises upward toward heaven. We are the point where these two universes intersect. What we do, matters. Our hands, our feet, our words and our motions are all-important. No deed goes unnoticed. No act is too small or irrelevant to not be of consequence. Everything is a connection to something else. Every action taken does not occur in a vacuum, it has a ripple effect.

There is a reason that we, of all creatures, have been made in the image of God. Our willful or ignorant acts cause an untold, unending chain of reactions that will ultimately wend its way throughout the cosmos. God is attentive. So is nature. In fact, Kabbalists are so attuned to this idea that whenever they are about to perform a conscious act of God's will, they first pray, "May this act that I perform be worthy in the sight of the Almighty and cause a healing in the universe...".

Reflect.

"Woe to the person who thinks that these stories are just stories...." *Zohar*

Chapter 8

Expectations: Your Worst Enemy

> In meditations from night visions
> When a deep sleep falls upon man
> Terror called to me and I shuddered
> It terrorized my bones
> A spirit passed by me
> And made the hair on my body stand on end... ***Job 4:13-15***

In our imagination, what is the worst possible thing that could happen to us? What is our darkest, most fearsome nightmare? What form do the demons take? What do these nocturnal visions look like? In the coming chapter we are going look at where some of the deepest, most frightening pain originates. There is a dark space where our fears reside. If we do not try to understand how our fears affect us, how can we ever hope to conquer them? Therefore we will confront our nightmare directly. We begin with Job.

Job is surely the most complex and difficult of biblical books. Perhaps *terrifying* is a better description. The story inverts everything we know about life. It takes the sacred beliefs that we hold with deep fervency and stands them on their head. It takes our hope and throttles it. What we have been taught since we were first capable of understanding thought is that life is linear: all things proceed in a standard, organized way. Kindness is rewarded and evil is punished. Good things happen to good people, bad things happen to bad people. Through the years of our lives, this idea has been ingrained into our consciousness. Parents, schools, and bosses have underlined that same ideal: Good things happen when we are good.

The book of Job challenges and undermines that belief. Job teaches that pain is senseless, meaningless; life is almost a roulette game of random chance. Life, health and prosperity are like game pieces in a Monopoly board. They move according to the throw of the dice. Can this really be a book of the Bible?

Job is the story of a righteous man who fears God, does the right thing and winds up in ruin, despite his devout faith. We helplessly watch as good Job is reduced to a pathetic state: He is stripped of family, house and possessions. For no apparent reason, this decent man is reduced to sitting in ashes, body swollen with lesions and boils.

Normally, in any religious text we would expect a man to suffer because he needs to learn a lesson. While reading his story we wonder if perhaps Job is really evil; maybe he is guilty of some great atrocity. Maybe he lives the outward life of a saint while covering up some secret part of his life. Or maybe, the righteous need to suffer more than those who stand on shakier faith? For them, it is a refinement of character, a deepening of belief. Yet, throughout the book we are constantly reminded that Job's pain is without cause; it is arbitrary. In fact - just in case we overlook the point- the opening verses of Job announces to the reader that Job was absolutely "flawless."

In all religious traditions there is a wrestling with why God allows/makes gross injustices to happen. If we look hard enough, there are invariably reasonable answers for suffering; some hidden fault, a past crime, even a purposeful cleansing of character. Working through our pain, we experience a catharsis, a washing away of iniquity. In the end, we emerge stronger and more devout. We suffer because we need, or sometimes even deserve, to suffer.

For the soulful reader who tries to understand Job, the question is not academic. If we take the story seriously, it matters a great deal to find out why righteous Job suffers. The tale certainly makes interesting reading. But the soul wants to know its underlying message. How do we understand the miserable things that happen to this man?

What do we make of reward and punishment?

It is not the standard tale of reward and punishment. The book is unlike any other. We want simplicity; we yearn for straight-forward answers to life. We want to know that righteousness is rewarded and evil is punished. In opening up the book of Job we expect to see the real reason behind suffering. To our amazement, the figure called Job is unconcerned with the question, 'How do I assign blame for my suffering?' Instead, the seeker of truth is brought to ask another question, 'How do we live in a world where bad things happen to decent people and still retain our faith in a universe that is balanced? For many, the deepest unspoken fear is that there is no compensation for our acts. The good work we do goes unnoticed. Can this possibly be true? And, if it is true, how do we maintain faith in God which encourages and wants us to be good when reward is not promised?' That is the book's underlying quandary.

The ancient sages said, "Job never was. There was no such person." If the story is not a historical fact, how do we read it? How is to be understood? As a parable? A metaphor? If so, what is the purpose of this terrifying book? The answer to that question may be even more disturbing than if Job actually lived.

A significantly more difficult question is aimed at the reader: How is our inner spiritual life affected by the story of Job-the-pious? In other words, if we were Job, how would we begin to approach and understand God? How could we live a religious existence knowing that life is indifferent to our cries of anguish and callous to the painful sob of human outrage? What do we discern from Job's tale of suffering? What do we extrapolate from our suffering? Where is the salvation in Job's awful pain? Where can we find redemption for ourselves in Job's suffering?

The ultimate question for Job is not to determine who is righteous and who is evil. The story is not even about how God deals with His servant Job. That question is skillfully avoided by the author of Job through the long narrative. Instead, it is a tale about how a man responds to his afflictions. The reason why the story is so frightening is because it is so real. We do not read Job to understand Job. We read the book to understand us.

I like baseball. Mostly, I enjoy games where I can see both the ball and players, which generally excludes the professional games of the major leagues. So, I try to attend minor league baseball games where the whole human drama is revealed before my eyes. I can actually see the pitcher spit, the restless movement of the left fielder and the spotty green infield.

Sometimes in the minor leagues the best parts of the game are played not on the field but in the stands. On one particular day, arriving just after the start of the game as I was about to enter the stadium, I heard a commotion. People were shouting from the rafters. I saw arms pointing and heard voices yelling something I could not make out. Following the direction of their hands, I jogged a few yards to my right where there lay a ball on the grass that had been "fouled" by a batter.

"Throw it to me!" I heard ten different voices shout from above. They held up their mitts gesturing for me to send the prize into their waiting hands. "Me!" "Me!"

I picked up the ball and turned to walk back toward the line of people waiting to get into the stadium thinking about my small triumph. As a kid, my father took me to some games at Fenway Park in Boston. I would bring my glove each time in the hope that I would be the one to catch the lucky foul ball. A few times, balls came within a few rows of me. But, I never came back from a game with a baseball. Until now.

Congratulating myself on a lucky day, I saw a little boy – maybe six or seven years old, turning the corner from behind me. His little legs running, and mouth panting from having followed me. I gestured for him to stop, cup his hands together. He stood motionless and followed my instructions. I then lobbed the baseball toward him. He scooped it up and ran away smiling.

The crowd above in the stadium turned back to the game, disappointed. The boy scooted back to his parents, eyes on his ball.

As I returned to my place in line, a young man with a smile approached me, "You know, you made my son's day." He turned and walked off. I was right. It was my lucky day.

Moral of the story? Find a kid and do something nice for him? No.

Moral of the story? Expect people to give heartfelt thanks for our good deeds? No.

The only sustainable moral is that having no expectations makes each moment a precious gift. Had I been waiting for a thank-you, it is likely that I would have experienced a disappointing let-down. After all, why didn't the father say more about how I helped his son? Why such a terse thanks? What if he said nothing at all? My efforts would have been for nothing. I would have ended up without a baseball <u>and</u> feeling like an idiot. The expectation of thanks could have destroyed the moment, ruined my day. Imagine the potential for anger with expectations of what we feel we are owed.

Perhaps what Job's story is presenting is a grownup perspective of life. The narrative is coarse and difficult but points to the most mature view of how life operates. The story weans us away from the belief that good is always rewarded and sin punished. The greatest theology is like the greatest love: we do it because we want to do it. Without expecting something in return, we simply act out of love.

Gifts can be a major problem. Frankly, you may not like the color or the size is way off. But you know from experience that if you say, "Thanks for thinking about me but I really do not need this," that they are going to cry or start fuming about what an ingrate you are. Their expectation for having given the gift is that they receive something in return. That is not a gift given freely with an open heart. It is a gift with an expectation of gratitude.

How many times have people said, "I'll never send them another birthday card. They never remember me!" Such thinking is destructive. It eats away at our tendency towards goodness. It consumes part of us. It can destroy relationships. It might even destroy them! There are people who harbor this kind of angst until their death. Relationships are ruptured because of such incidental expectations.

I remember a sermon I gave many years ago about the need to make amends with family. "At all costs, find a way to open dialogue," I urged. "It does not matter who was right or wrong. Does it really settle anything if you were absolutely correct and they were dead wrong? The utter pain of estrangement between brothers affects you more than it hurts them. Be selfish! Why hurt yourself? Maybe the greatest selfish thing you can ever do is forgive them just for the sake of freeing yourself of carrying that burdensome load! The only thing that really matters is healing the raw, open wounds of the past."

It was a sermon I delivered in the aftermath of a very painful argument I had with my sister. We were not speaking. The fight happened about one month before the sermon. Every day since our argument was agony. The awful pain gnawed at me every day. I could not get rid of the recurring words we exchanged in that last conversation/argument. She accused me. I yelled at her. Replaying that terrible scene kept me up every night for weeks. Afterwards, I thought about the things I should have said. I considered what I ought to have countered with. Endlessly analyzing her every statement, I found myself growing angrier and more indignant with every day. It was hell.

Finally, I decided that enduring this hell was not worth it to me. I gathered up my courage to call and apologize. I told her that she meant more to me than I had ever expressed before. I needed her. She just cried. Although separated by some three thousand miles, a wonderful thing happened that night when I set aside my pride.

The stories I heard in the aftermath of the sermon when I spoke about my fight, the anger, the estrangement and ultimately the reconciliation with my sister were remarkable. I received telephone calls and many letters... some came even years later. In one long, hand-written letter from a congregant I learned of two brothers who had not spoken for years. They were able to reconnect because one of them that heard the sermon recognized himself in the story. He dropped his ego and telephoned his brother. Neither one could remember why they stopped talking years before! Each laughed and cried as they hung up continents apart and hearts reconnected.

Another member, Jim, called his sister and said directly, "I don't know what went wrong but I heard my rabbi speak over the holidays and suddenly realized that so much time has passed. I have missed you. We could have spent birthdays together. Our children could have grown up visiting with one another, playing in each other's homes. All that time was lost! I do not even know what your kids look like or what they are doing or whether they like vanilla ice cream. I don't know what went wrong," he cried, "but I love you. Can I come back into your life?"

In another case, a son called his estranged father and arranged to meet in the coming months. For years, the two had not spoken. It was like a toxic boil that someone needed the courage to burst and allow healing to begin. I have kept many of those letters in my file about reconciled family members who were able to forgive past hurts without any thought of gain...but they did gain much in the process. I suspect that the prime reason why people do not make amends is because they cannot anticipate that their rapprochement will be returned. They fear that they words of reconciliation will be spurned. Expecting an outcome immobilizes us from doing the right thing. If we were not afraid of failure, imagine what we could be capable of doing!

In my family there is an outstanding hero. Aunt Hilda. Aunt Hilda used to send birthday cards to everybody. She never missed a date. Hilda carefully jotted down each person's special day; children, siblings, nieces, nephews, grandchildren, great nieces and nephews. Aunt Hilda would buy and address the card with about one month to spare, just in case something happened. God forbid, she thought, the card did not get out in time. I always got my card on time.

Her husband eventually died and Aunt Hilda developed Alzheimer's. Afterward, Hilda's daughter found a small pile of cards on her mother's dresser that were written, addressed and even stamped as she had prepared them in advance of birthdays…just in case.

I wonder how many people knew Aunt Hilda's birthday and returned the favor of being remembered? Certainly she would have been inundated for the goodness she dispensed so liberally to others. But, I suspect, it never really mattered to her because Aunt Hilda was one of those rare individuals who did what her heart told her because that was what she did. The fact that Aunt Hilda sent out cards certainly made her unusual but what made her most special and the true hero that she was, was the fact she had no expectations from the ones she sent greetings to. That is why she was a hero.

A gift given with an expectation behind it is not really a gift at all. The gift, predicated on a response, is an exchange, not a gift. From somewhere came the insane idea that when we give something, we have the right to expect a "gift" in return. That is not a gift. A real gift has no strings attached to it. That is what the book of Job is trying to warn us about.

Expecting life to be kind, expecting it to reward us for our good actions, supports the naïve childhood belief in absolute justice. This kind of thinking will only lead to pain and disappointment. No good can come of it. The ancient ones warned us, "Do not be like the servant who waits upon the Master expecting a reward…" for such thinking leads to despair.

Example: A distraught woman once approached the holy man,

Baal Shem Tov. Crying and full of anguish, she begged the miracle man to appeal to the Holy of Holies that she would bear a child. Listening attentively, full of compassion for the poor woman, the Baal Shem Tov took off his cloak and gave it to her. "Wear this cloak," he instructed "and good things will happen." The next year she gave birth to a beautiful child.

As often happens, history repeats itself. When another woman, tired and bitter from trying to have a child, came to a disciple of the Baal Shem Tov, he did not know what to do. So he repeated the tale of the Baal Shem Tov's cloak. The woman instantly brightened. "Then all we have to do is find the holy coat!" she exclaimed.

"No," replied the wise man. "That was her story, not yours.

Each person has their own tale and passage through life. Her story is not your story. Your story is not mine. We cannot expect what happened to one person to happen to us. That story belongs only to them...

Think back to childhood. What most people remember about being young are the feelings of unabashed awe at the world. The pond is a vast ocean. The tiny cottage is an endless maze of passageways and hidden cabinets. Everything is larger than life. A man dressed up as a duck from a comic book is an amazing character that we can nuzzle against and hug. All life is amazing and real!

What we possessed as a child was an openness to the world that was not prejudiced by expectations. This is the real gem from our younger days; the youthful exuberance of the whole embrace of the universe without nagging doubts about conspiracy theories and deception. What happened? The world never stopped being awesome. It is as it was. What changed? *We stopped being open and full of awe.* Instead, we started demanding that life compensate us for our acts.

In the holy city of Safed, the servant of the Kabbalah, the holy Ari, uttered, "One must pray secluding oneself with the Holy One. You must speak with the Lord with quiet fear, as a slave speaks to a master or a child to his father." Recreating that initial child-like awe of the world is a fundamental building block to the highest levels to reaching God.

Our story is unique. The passage of our life is one-of-a-kind.

Each moment contains the seeds of redemption but can only be seen through the lens of awe, witnessing this time as a unique event, never to be repeated. That is why the coat could only work once. The story illustrates that there is no panacea to our pain. Sometimes there is no cure for our cancer. The only possession that Job never lost was his awe; his deep appreciation for whatever came into his field of vision. Like the old woman who was poor and had lost all her teeth but two. She said, "Thank God these two teeth are opposite each other. That way I can still chew my food." Every breath is a wondrous gift. Each act in our life is the first time this has happened since the inception of the universe. There is no template for human action and reaction. Everything is a first. Eden could not be closer.

The Zohar informs us, "Since the holy Temple has been razed, the only avenue open to us to reach God is through prayer." Just as no animal was like the previous one, just as the blood of one being contains DNA unique to it, just as the incantation of the High Priest happened only once, so too, each prayer must be the only prayer. If this is true, there can never be any expectations, for expectations are an indication that this has happened before.

There is an apt illustration in an old tale about a scholar and a jeweler. Coming from different perspectives, each sees the world in a dissimilar light. One looks at the rocks and sees diamonds. The other gazes at the sky and finds incalculable wealth. The diamonds are meaningless to him just as the constellations mean nothing to the other. Not only do they see the physical world differently from one another but also find fulfillment in a distinct way.

A jeweler approached a famed Talmudic figure. The sage asked the jeweler to show him his most valuable possessions. The gemologist took out his bag of diamonds and deliberately emptied them onto the table. "Tell me about them," the sage then asked.

The jeweler then proceeded to point out to his teacher diamonds of various hues, shapes and sizes indicating the worth of each gem.

"And this," he said pulling out one diamond from near the bottom of the pile is my choice diamond. It alone is worth 5,000 silver pieces!"

The venerable sage gazed at it and said, "It looks just like the rest."

He smiled knowingly. "You see, my teacher, you have to be an expert to really understand their value."

"I suppose you must be right," considered the sage. "It all looks the same to me because I am surrounded by lustrous gems of a different sort so there is nothing that I lack."

Let's review.

To be open to fear, awe, ecstatic joy is to be fully alive. The lesson imparted by Job is priceless for it teaches us the most profound lesson of life: Stop expecting life to be fair or unfair. That is a path of self-destruction. Stop expecting anything from life.

Expectations only lead to disappointment. Determining that we already know what will happen is the most self-limiting thing we can do to ourselves. Basically we shackle our feelings to a pole in the ground that severely limits how far we can travel from the stave. Those shackles allow us to venture so far, and no further. We place ourselves into a self-constructed and self-limiting hell every time we hold expectations. There is no way of yet determining human reaction or the future; therefore it is in our hands to just do the right thing and then open our eyes and hearts without expectation of return or reward.

A liberation, a breathtaking joy comes from being receptive to the new-and-never-to-be-repeated now. That real freedom can only emerge from not waiting for our expectations to be fulfilled. The kind of thinking that waits for a thank-you or particular reaction is called the Road to Despair. Looking at Job's statement at the beginning of this chapter in this new light, we understand it in a new light (the brackets are the new reading of the text):

"It terrorized my bones [this is the fear that arises from expectations that have not and cannot be met]

A spirit passed by me [this is the great liberation from the expectation that goodness will be rewarded]

And made the hair on my body stand on end [in utter awe, we are free when we have freed ourselves]"

Approach life with openness to all things. Take time to look at the world as you once did, as a child. Embrace the light that comes to your eyes as the first rays of creation in the Garden. Think: this moment has never happened before and will never recur or be recaptured again. Spend a day, a week gazing at the universe as if you see it for the first time. The waters that lap at your toes will never look as tantalizing. The woods that beckon are filled with deep and great treasures of life and mystery. Be young before the brittleness of age has settled into your psyche. Expect nothing from your actions.

"Do not be like the servant who waits upon the Master expecting a reward…" When you give, just give without a desire of reward. Ironically, the absence of expectation creates its own reward.

Chapter 9

You and God

> The seed of prayer is an attachment to God.
>
> *--Rebbe Nachman*

P ay close attention. Although this chapter may look innocuous, a profound teaching is about to be proffered. We are going to gently dip our feet into the mystical waters of Kabbalah now. What we have learned so far is the backdrop to understand the rich gifts that Kabbalah offers. While the concepts are not difficult; do not be deceived, they are very deep.

Rebbe Nachman's statement comes from one of the greatest and most unknown, holiest people who ever lived. While his life was brief, Nachman's influence on the way people can be touched by God has laid the foundation for many generations of seekers yearning for something we all know exists but feel is too distant or too ethereal for us to claim. Rebbe Nachman had something very specific in mind when he used "attachment" (*devekute* in the original language).

Throughout the balance of this book I am going to use the Hebrew word in place of the English as is connotes something far more spiritually deep than mere attachment or connection. *Devekute* means something like 'inseparability' to Nachman. *Devekute* is an inseparable cleavage that comes out of a deep longing to be close to God. It is a determined and insatiable hunger that will only be filled by a connection with the Divine. An adoring love which has no description except to say that it is a feeling that cuts across all lines of peoples underlies the concept of *devekute*. It is an emotion that has no boundaries; a relationship whose desire reaches well beyond the realm of the physical.

Rebbe Nachman insisted that the whole concept is not beyond us, it lurks just beneath the surface ready to be embraced. In fact, the taste of *devekute* is so familiar that the very thought of it sends waves of recognition flooding, coursing through us. We **know** what it is. It is almost as if a part of us belongs to God and once we feel that connection with the One, our Self becomes whole. We all know what it feels like and would gladly give anything we possess to own it once again (Is there anyone who, when pressed, cannot come up with a defining moment in their life? A moment of Ilumination and calm understanding? Rebbe Nachman would tell us, that was a moment of *devekute* when we touched God). Even more, considering everything we have endured and learned throughout the years of our existence -- life and death, work and pleasure, family issues and the balance of what life offers-- what would it be worth to have **that** kind of peace and light last through the years of our lives? Not just a fleeting moment of grace?

Homo religiousis is the person whose soul is consumed with having once tasted that elixir and forever holds on to searching to recreate that sublime moment of connection. Once a person has touched the sacred essence of the Divine, they find that all life becomes comprehensible. With great clarity, we 'get it'. Our life makes sense. All the good and worthy discussions about our growing our 407K, the weather report, national deficit and even finding meaning in everyday life seem to fade into insignificance once the Ineffable has been tasted. The search is over. That which once engaged our most powerful and vigorous emotions- a corporate climb, the quest for truth, another height to surmount - now feels hollow against the breadth, the enormity of the Divine. One sublime moment, a mere second of feeling the touch of God, in an entire life, is enough to change us forever.

The burgeoning issue that we grapple with is how we choose to either integrate or compartmentalize this experience. Put simply, what do we do once we have experienced God? What happens to that moment of clarity? What do we do with it? It is simple to sip the elixir and then return back to our mundane functions. It is so easy to forget or dismiss because we are swiftly engulfed by the demands of the outer world. That once-tasted ultimate truth will then be converted into nostalgia or *devekute*.

Nostalgia can be neatly packed away into the recesses of our memory and taken out every now and again to make us smile as we recall the experience. Nostalgia is a memory or a feeling that we reference every now and again taking down from the shelf in our mind. On the opposite hand, the person who yearns for *devekute* can transform that "knowing" into a lifelong realization of the holiness of their soul. Unlike nostalgia, *devekute* is the driving hunger to repeat the meeting with God. Once a person has determined that *devekute* will be an integral part of their life, their relationship with themselves, others and the Holy One will never be the same.

Love, another reasonable translation for *devekute*, is surely the most powerful, palpable human force in the universe. It moves mountains and bridges chasms thought impassable. It instills meaning into eating, breathing, working, studying. With *devekute* there is an ultimate goal that drives our life. A question: Is it possible to feel love without love being tendered? Can you love God without first sensing the Divine flow of love coming from Him?

Devekute is reciprocal. In feeling the overwhelming sense of a timeless, eternal embrace, *devekute* seeks to invite the Other into that dynamic. One of the noblest leaders of this past century, Kalonymos Kalman Schapira said, "Not only does God hear our prayers, God prays through them as well." God is searching for us. *Devekute* is not unilateral; it is, by definition, bilateral. It comes from Above to enter our souls and pure love then emanates from below in an acknowledgement of the gift received and then enters into the Divine realm. If this is true, it seems that God needs us. Can this be possible? Does God need anything, least of all, us? We will soon look at this question but first the next step in our journey is learning how to bring that *devekute* out of our self and raising it to the level of a real attachment, love and then relationship. Yet we begin elsewhere, in another time, another place…

The narrative is short and begins here:

"These are the generations of Noah (Noah was a righteous man, perfect in his time; Noah walked with God). Noah had three sons: Shem, Ham and Yafet."

We tend to read the tale of Noah as a benign story about a bunch of animals in a towering ship. Darling visions of bunnies hopping in tandem up the gangway of the boat makes the story even more fun and entertaining. Lumbering rhinoceros make their way into the hold. A cacophony of sounds flows out of the vessel as the merry crew sails away on the tide. If we read the story with all its implications, an entirely different picture begins to emerge.

The chronicle of Noah opens a terrible chapter in the Bible. The biblical narration is silent about the suffering and pain of the drowning victims of the deluge. Yet, when the waters of the deep rush upward and meet the unyielding downpour from above, chaos happens. Animals excluded from the ark begin to feel the water pressure engulf their bodies and start fill their lungs. Entire civilizations shriek in utter terror. Their eyes see a slow, unavoidable death. All life in a prolonged tortuous end is extinguished in a terrifying gasp. We hear nothing of the terror as the waters rush to encompass all that breathes. There are no testimonies of the dead. To be caught in a vice as the waters from above close the gap to meet the waters below must have been horrible.

This part of the text must be as true as Noah laboring to build his ark. This aspect of the tale is not spoken. The terror must have occurred but the Bible does not even mention it. In fact, there is much more that the story does not reveal.

The Text also offers little information about even supposed germane aspects of the tale. For example, who was Noah? Where was he born? Why was he considered such a "righteous" man? Had he done something to warrant that description? Some scholars debate whether he was really even that saintly. After all, the Bible qualifies his goodness by saying that he was "perfect in *his* time." Does that mean he would be not quite perfect in another era? That Noah was 'as good as they get?' Or that Noah was "perfect in his time," despite the rampant evil around him?

All these questions should trouble us. At the heart of the story is something even more vexing. Why does this Biblical episode start out by stating that "These are the generations of Noah" and then immediately digress into what sounds like an apology by saying that he was righteous and perfect? Weren't we just talking about his "generations" not his qualities?? Where are his generations? What happened to them? Why does the Bible not go on to tell us who these "generations" are? There seems to be something missing from the text. Is the Writ corrupt? Perhaps the Bible means to apologize for what follows: "Noah had three sons." Could it be that a "perfect" man could raise inferior children? Is that the underlying message? Is that why there is something missing from the story? Noah's children were nothing to feel proud about?

The Kabbalists know that everything is real and at the same time a metaphor. Uncovering the metaphor reveals hidden depths. In this case, listen to how they understand this passage:

Text: "These are the generations of Noah"

Commentary: We give birth to our children. For most people, we will give birth to physical progeny, children. There is another different kind of birthing, though. A universal birthing can take place where no children are involved. In this instance, we give birth to another kind of generation. We have the ability to generate life, possibility, death, curse, humility, blessing, pride….. In fact, our days are a never-ending string generating healing and pain. With our words, for example, we unleash limitation. How often I have heard the cry of a child in a store only to be followed by a fierce tirade of a threatening parent. "You shut up now or I'll really give you something to cry about!" Or, "just wait until I get you home!" The sound of a sharp slap of hand against skin. The child is silent.

Who knows what would happen to the child if the parent had taken another approach? If the parent were to speak to the child with kindness? Or listen to them to determine if there was a legitimate gripe? Who can foretell the repercussions of that interaction? How will the child grow up with the memory of those events?

A similar is repeated every time we speak or interact with another human being. Every action creates generations. Throughout our days we are equipped to generate a positive flow of energy. A thoughtful word to the clerk; a thanks to the employee for going out of their way to help us can have a powerful effect. It may change the way they treat their next customer by being more caring and deliberate with their needs. On the other hand, a complaint about how they stock their shelves or even something as innocuous as blowing the car's horn at someone can cause a long chain reaction of negative events. Who can predict the reaction of the driver who hears the impatient horn behind him shouting out to move more quickly? Will they go home and uncoil their anger at their family? Perhaps take it out on the next available underling? All these instances, positive and negative, are kinds of generations.

Every person is the source of infinite generation. Each physical and non-physical communication that is placed into the world creates endless ripples. It may only be a tiny pebble that we cast into the water, but the reverberations of throwing that stone are unknown. The ripples spread out in wider and wider circles until they eventually touch the edge of the pond. Even the frogs bristle at the current we set in motion. Fish move against it. Other currents are caught against what we caused putting into play further changes into this contained space. The universe is our pond. No action ever takes place in a vacuum. In a poetic sense, each ripple that we initiate is a "child" that we have birthed.

We move in repetitive ways. The expressions that we use, the motions we employ, the looks we give, the tasks we perform; all this is a part of a great mosaic which more than likely recurs with startling regularity. Few, if any of us, are so free from neurotic behavior, so inventive that our words, actions and reactions that we are anything but predictable. Seen like this, our life is a repeating pattern of sequences. Most of us have set in motion untold generations or ripples in the world while never conscious of what we have started. So repetitive are our modalities of behavior that we often do not even realize what we create or that we have been the catalyst for anything.

Perhaps then Noah's *generations* can be viewed as emanations or projections of his self. Seeing the story of Noah with this nuanced interpretation, "These are the generations of Noah, [who was essentially] a righteous man, perfect in his time… Noah had three generations: Shem (which connotes the Name), Ham (indicates heat) and Yafet (meaning 'beauty')." Each of these named generations could be understood as a ripple -- not a son, but nonetheless a "child." The three generations of Noah are metaphors for the emanations that Noah set into motion. These

122

three ripples were the gifts which Noah placed into our world.

Understood like this, Noah gifted the universe with godliness (Shem - again, this means Name and refers to the Divine One). This was his first "generation." After so many years of human dissociation with God, Noah restored a sense of connection with the Divine One. One of Noah's generations was a great contribution to his contemporaries and heirs. He reintroduced God to the living. At the same time, Noah also birthed an attribute carried by his predecessors (Ham - heat is reactionary and potentially explosive, and wonderfully effusive) and depth (Yafet - beauty is a metaphor for altruistic behavior). What the Bible wants us to notice is that these three ripples entered and permanently altered the world. It would never be the same again. Thousands of years later we are still pulled by the resonances of these Noah's generations.

The kabbalists provide alternative names for these three generations of Noah. They are: *neshama* (soul), *ruach* (spirit) and *nefesh* (body). Each aspect is holy but they represent different levels of spiritual growth in humanity. Starting at the lowest rung, *nefesh* is what makes us human. In the image of God, *nefesh* is the vessel which can be filled with anything we see fit to place in it. The *nefesh* is a waiting, open receptacle. In fact, this is how the Bible labels the first being in the Garden. Once the Divine Breath has blown into this being, the Text states that it became a "living *nefesh*." At birth, just like creation, this same vessel awaits opportunity to be infused with goodness. Anxious for an opportunity to fulfill the Will, the *nefesh* searches out the next stage, *ruach*, to fill that space and complete the person.

Ruach is that essential matter which existed even before Creation. Its existence dates back well before the formation of the *nefesh*. The *ruach* is that which "blew across the waters" in the earliest passages of Genesis. A part of God, the ruach pre-existed humanity. The second time we hear that word is when the Creator blows "*ruach*" into the still *nefesh* of the empty being in Eden. *Ruach* is the spirited animating factor of life. It is the breathing, pulsating energy which allows us to reach beyond the physical realm. It is the holy breath that resonates in every human being since Adam. There is a *knowing* part of us that offers us a taste of the sublime. This is *ruach*.

The *nefesh* and *ruach* are two sorts of generations, gifts of Noah, that have been passed down to us as characteristics that operate optimally when they work together. Can a body exist separate or independent from the spirit? Yes and, I suspect, we all know people who have resisted the joining of those forces. There is a discernable emptiness about them. They are like vapor. The *ruach* cannot be perverted, but it can be ignored. The voice of that which is "right" can be shunted aside as if it does not exist. For example, there would be no reason to have laws if people were not tempted to ignore the voice of goodness. Ruach is ever-present but can be silenced. We have the ability to cordon off the voice of *ruach* so that we only access our nefesh when making decisions about what is good for us

The highest state of being is that of the *neshama*. This level cannot be reached until the lower two, *nefesh* and *ruach*, have been conjoined. The *neshama* simply cannot be attained until we have readied ourselves for that event. That is why Ham and Yafet, progeny of Noah and aspects of the self, must be learned and absorbed. They are the first steps that lead to higher level.

A brief review: The tale of Noah is not just a story to entertain, a lesson on the history of humanity or even teach something as important as morality. Rather, it possesses the hidden message of the breakdown of the human spirit into three steps or levels. Through those levels the Bible reveals the ultimate potential of every person. We are cast in the "image of God" with a reach that far exceeds anything we have approximated in our lives. Each of us can learn the great lesson from Noah about the primary components of our spirit that can allow us to become the fulfillment of our dreams.

Here come the deepest questions: What do we desire? *Devekute*? Proximity to God? A sense of absolute understanding of self and world? A pervasive and powerful desire to be in the Divine embrace? A contentment with self? Do we yearn for a consuming connection to God and a living organic relationship with the world? If your responses are yes, this is where we begin our real work.

Everything we have learned up to this point has been an exercise in preparing for this next step. I therefore suggest that now is a time to pause and recall and re-read any of the previous chapters that have been difficult or obscure. Try them again.

A house is built upon a foundation. These prior segments have put into place the foundation stone upon which we stand. From that vantage we construct our inner edifice. If needed, please go back and review.

Chapter 10

Nefesh

"Give truth to Jacob; loving-kindness to Abraham." --*Micah*
Why would the holy Bible tell us that one thing needs to be given to Abraham, another to Jacob? Because each needed something different to become whole. Abraham required Laws, stricture, so that he could make sense of a random universe where he had no teacher. The other required faith to make him whole. Abraham had abundant faith, Jacob followed the commandments. There are two kinds of fear. One is fear of punishment; the other is fear of heaven.

-Rebbe Nachman

Truth joined with justice creates the ultimate faith - *Zohar*

We are about to enter the realm where the lower and higher self become united to form an integrated whole. Perhaps one of the most insidious dangers of life is living a splintered existence. Like the forefathers, Jacob and Abraham, we need to access all parts of our being. At all costs, we must strive to be whole. It does no good to disown any part of our self. Incorporating and accepting every aspect of our being is integral, critical to becoming whole.

A Tale of Two Men

Early in Genesis (chapter 12), the Lord appears to Abram and tells him, "Go unto yourself." Now, this command by God is usually interpreted as "Go and travel to Canaan…" but the words are too complex to mean that. The Kabbalah rightly observes that the command literally means, "Go unto yourself." In other words, 'seek out what is missing from you so that you can be truly whole.'

Abram set out to follow the Divine Command and discover who he was. What did he find? According to the Kabbalah, Abram used his gift of truth to bring much goodness to the Promised Land. Truth was the tool that Abram utilized to respond to the needs of others. Abram changed the landscape of Canaan by bringing integrity to the inhabitants of the place. He was honest in his commerce, careful with his weights, deliberate with his words. The people listened intently to him. They learned from his actions. His only tool was truth which he used to teach the inhabitants of the land. An even more profound moment was when Abram discovered his inborn ability to change the world through his actions.

"Give loving-kindness to Abraham," was what Abram achieved at the moment he understood the path of his life. Truth was his hallmark but loving-kindness would ultimately make Abram whole. At that moment, the patriarch became whole and God changed his name to reflect his newfound self; Abraham.

Jacob, on the other hand, needed truth to become whole. He waited until his brother Esau was exhausted from the hunt. For Esau, it was an unsuccessful day. It had been an unbearably long, frustrating day of chasing prints in the earth, listening to the sounds of the forest and sitting still for endless hours. Many times Esau found the mark, stealthily crept towards the prey and every time they escaped his arrows. He was frustrated, angry and worn out. Now, at the edge of collapse, Esau sniffs the wind. He smells and deeply inhales the air of food cooking. A thick, savory stew makes his mouth burn with released saliva. Esau moves toward the scent. In the clearing, he finds his brother bent over a cauldron. Jacob exacts a price for the lentil stew; he asks for Esau's birthright.

Years later, as Father Isaac lay dying, Jacob dons a disguise to fool the old blind man. Pretending to be Esau, Jacob approaches his father's bedside and asks to receive what he negotiated from Esau, the blessing of the firstborn. Jacob lies to his father. "I am Esau," Jacob tells the old man. "Bless me." Two hearts are broken.

"Give truth to Jacob," because that is what he needs to be whole.

Abraham and Jacob need different things. Until Abraham seeks and embraces loving-kindness and Jacob embodies the truth that he needs, neither man will be complete. They must both approach the physical universe treading the steps that are meant for them to follow.

Abraham Joshua Heschel once remarked that "needs are spiritual opportunities." Although it may sound lofty, Heschel is simply telling us that whenever we need something, that *need* can give birth to a longing and ultimately a connection to God. We must therefore latch onto the need. In owning our neediness, we better reach out to God with a fervency that can expand our soul. The *want* creates an intense and powerful connection. So much of our spiritual life hinges on wanting, needing. The hunger that we harbor along with the physical practices mentioned previously, is enough to open the door to the next stage of spiritual growth. The only tool we require is the want, the desire.

Nefesh implies an awareness of the world. That is because our *nefesh* is connected to this world. It observes, participates and interacts. It is the ground of our being. It is our physical presence. While sometimes the *nefesh* is all that some people will ever realize—there is much more as we will soon learn -- it is nonetheless where all spiritual journeys must begin. We begin at the beginning; the *nefesh*.

We are not souls that exist independent of our bodies and Kabbalah's goal is not to tease them apart from one another. To the contrary, Kabbalah seeks to seamlessly connect them so that we are not fragmented people.

The Bible dictates that we care for the *nefesh* and be attentive to its needs. That is why there are statements found in the Bible which speak about "not marking the skin," and not "defacing the body," and not "rounding the corners of one's hair." It is implied that anything which negatively impacts or destroys the body's image is likewise prohibited. For example, afflicting the body as an unnecessary appendage has no place in the Writ. Now you might ask; who would do such a thing? Throughout history, ascetics have punished their bodies or ignored its needs. They wanted to divest themselves of the love for their body as a means to rise to higher spiritual levels. Running against this theme is the idea that the *nefesh* is a gift of God and carries holiness.

The purpose of life is not to dismiss, ignore or minimize the *nefesh*. The *nefesh* is supposed to be used in concert with all the other dimensions of the self; it is the gateway to personal growth.

You cannot pray unless you exist. While this may sound rather obvious, it is an important idea to keep in mind: you are the beginning and God is the end. Nonetheless, **you** are the starting point. Acknowledging existence is essential to the task of reaching outward. It, like a simile mentioned previously, represents the basement or foundation of the structure we are building. Do not be misled: The fact that it is the basement does not mean that it is unimportant. Not only do the upper levels depend upon its strength but, as you will see, it is a powerful force by itself. That is why the body is not just a container, it is a holy vessel. We cannot possibly hope to reach any other level without an abiding acknowledgement and respect for it. There are, just in case we missed the point, numerous laws in the Bible that relate to care of the body or, more specifically, how not to abuse it.

Among the preparations for prayer is an important reference to the self. We started earlier with the point of light that is you.

A prayer. Blessed is the One in whose infinite wisdom has created hollow passageways, orifices of the body.

It is revealed and discerned only before the all-knowing Mind that if a single one of these myriad passageways should shut down, become obstructed, it would be impossible to exist.*

*A traditional prayer to be recited each time that a person relieves themselves of potentially deadly toxins, i.e. every time we void.

A deeply contemplative elderly man in my congregation, Sidney, was familiar with this prayer. He was brought up in a religious household and his father insisted that every time he visit the bathroom that he say the prayer after washing his hands and exiting. Now beyond seventy years, Sidney had recited these familiar words countless times. He could probably recite them in his sleep. Sidney lay in the Intensive Care Unit of the hospital as I came to visit him. Monitors arrayed around his bed were blinking and bleeping, an i.v. drip coursed it slow path through his veins. I stood by my old friend and clasped his hand.

"It's good to see you dear Sidney. Everyone has missed you back home. Frankly, we are like a puzzle with a piece missing. You are needed there. I have regards and love and more prayers than I can remember from all your friends. They all said the same thing: 'Tell Sid to get back here quick!'"

Sid began to cry. Creased by deep lines, tears trickled over his face and dripped down over his pillow and onto his chest.

Turning away from me, Sidney said, "You know, all my life, I said a prayer. Whenever I go to the toilet I say the words of thanks. My dad made me before I could even read. Since I was a tot, I would say those words. Until now, I think never really understood it. Maybe I just never appreciated it. I said the prayer because I was told to say it. Now, look at me. I am here in the ICU and could be dead because of one tiny malfunction in these miles of veins and arteries that run through this body." He looked down at the white sheet wrapping his body.

"One small obstruction almost killed me! I will never take this prayer for granted again. God does miracles every moment that I am alive. Through the course of saying the prayer for so many decades it had long since ceased being a prayer of meaning to me; it had become rote. Never again. I know what it means now."

Found near the beginning of every traditional morning service, this prayer feels so base, so elemental, that it is often overlooked. It is contains none of the usual eloquent statements and grand human-divine aspirations. There are no "great's" or "glorious'" or "hallelu-jah's." It is simply a thanksgiving prayer for moving one's bowels. What could be more grounded than that? It is a prayer of and for the *nefesh*. Where the ground of being meets the self is sated with power. This is where the ladder of heaven first touches the earth and stretches out to the highest heights, inviting us to climb upward.

The mystical Zohar likens the *nefesh* to a "shoe." The other layers of the self neatly slide into the "shoe" and housed there throughout our life's passage. The *nefesh* of a human being is the protective cover for what lies beneath. Just as a shoe gives shields the foot from sharp and harmful elements, so too the *nefesh* serves a vital function in carrying and protecting the soul. In fact, the description of the casting of the first man's body from the clay in the Garden of Eden is understood as the creation of this "shoe." The *nefesh* may not be the highest or most brilliant part of who we are but it is definitely the starting point where spirituality begins.

The journey to meet oneself begins with an acknowledgement of the value of the self, the *nefesh*. The wonder of life is the beginning of the process of being awake and aware. No thing and no one is worthless, no matter how small or insignificant it may appear.

This book began with the idea that we are great consumers of wisdom, tirelessly pursuing more and more knowledge. The Bible is clear about the value of knowledge. It indicates that knowledge for the sake of amassing more knowledge or for the sake sharpening one's own skill is of limited value. Only when applied to a noble cause does it become significant.

"The beginning of all wisdom is awe," states the Bible. True understanding of the world's knowledge commences with incredulity, a feeling of amazement. The wide-eyed wonder that we bring to a table laden with food with all its decorous colors and many smells gives a deep appreciation of the meal. Consuming the food is only a part of the experience. Afterward, what that nourishment does for our body is equally compelling. Is it not incredible the way anti-bodies protect us from harm? They run through us seeking out and destroying potentially harmful forces that would ravage the body. When we approach existence with a sense of anticipation and wonder, not only are we standing at the great portal of wisdom but open to the fullest appreciation of life.

In a conversation with a neurosurgeon, I asked him, "How much do we really understand about the brain?" He answered, "A fraction of a percent. The brain is an amazing organ whose secrets are largely shielded from our sights. We understand more and more through time but given the overall composition of the brain we know almost nothing. All we basically know is how to poke and prod. It is a very primitive understanding. And frankly, if that is not enough to make someone a believer in God, I don't know what is...."

One of the wisest people of this past century was a scion of a religious family that went back to illustrious roots from the Old Country as well as being a gifted philosopher, Abraham Joshua Heschel. He wrote:

> Awe is a way of being in rapport with the mystery of all reality. The awe that we sense or ought to sense when standing in the presence of a human being is a moment of intuition for the likeness of God which is concealed in his essence. Not only man; even inanimate things exist in a relation to the Creator. The secret of every being is the divine care and concern that are invested in it. Something sacred is at stake in every event. - *God in Search of Man*

Awe is the opposite of boredom. Boredom is dissociation of our soul to the world. It makes us bystanders in the universe. Boredom makes us passive observers. Everything becomes predictable and therefore mundane. In a word, boring. The older we become, the more facile it is to yawn at life before turning over and returning to our waking slumber; a mechanistic, almost robotic, approach to life. Through this monochromatic lens, our attention is fixed only on aberrations of nature. We seek out the freakish side of life and are drawn to them. Everything else brings on a stifled yawn.

Gauging the racy nature of television and movies, it is pretty evident that we, as a society, are bored. Each new show has to outdo the previous one with special effects, nudity, raunchiness and suggestion. What began as simple reality programs have leapt into the world of embarrassment as a form of entertainment. One person's shame and undoing has become a national pastime. We are bored.

On the other hand is amazement; the recognition that even a leaf is a testament to the vast, endless reach of God and life. Clouds gathering together, blowing overhead to form patterns that jump, dance and make us smile, are remarkable. A squirrel climbing a tree, a newly sprouted bud, electricity transformed into light, or an earthworm's slow progress can be riveting. Inherent in everything that exists is our ability to relate to it, appreciate its value and rejoice in its being. The *nefesh* is fed by awe. It is nourished by an appreciation of all that is.

Hayim of Krosno was walking with his students as they were discussing holy, lofty thoughts. Suddenly, the master paused and watched as a man above them walking on a tightrope between two buildings. Hayim was transfixed by the delicate balance the man maintained as he made his way across the thin strip of wire.

His students, in the meanwhile, were equally dumbfounded by the distraction of their teacher. "What is so important about this circus performer that you stopped listening to us?" they asked.

"I am amazed," said Hayim. "Here is a man risking his life walking across a tightrope forty feet above the ground. I am certain he is not thinking about the reward that is waiting for him on the other side. I am also sure that he does not see us, hear us, or even know that we are below him. He is not thinking about three steps from now or two or even his next step. That man is only thinking about this moment, where his foot touches the wire now. I am sure he is not even aware of his body, just where he stands at this moment."

Isn't that the powerful recognition? Just to be aware of where we stand right now? Not weighted down by what lies in the past (it is arguable that it is even in the past if it still occupies space in our present mind)? Not transfixed by what lies in front of us (as we all know from experience life has a way of not turning out as we anticipate)? Paying attention to where we are now is what Hayim saw and envied. That total experience of life is more than enough to satisfy our senses. No other form of distraction or entertainment is necessary to feel the flow of life in our veins. To be alive is enough.

Idea: The Sabbath is a key element that figures in the Bible and in every religion. At its core lies a crucial but hidden idea. In Exodus 31, there is the phrase "and on the seventh day He rested." While unremarkable in English, the original Hebrew text is highly revealing. The word "rest" in its usual form is not used here. The word employed by the Bible here for "rest" is a form of the word *nefesh*, the human capsule. A more close interpretation of that same phrase ought to read, "And on the seventh day he will become a nefesh."

Countless generations of Sages have pointed to this anomalous usage of the word *nefesh* and have said that it is not a mistake. The Bible is not overly concerned with our getting enough sleep. There are no heavenly ordinances commanding humanity to go to bed. To understand Exodus 31 in that way is to misinterpret what it wants us to understand. The Sabbath actually has nothing to do with our conception of "rest."

That passage is urging us to use one-seventh of our week, the Sabbath, to reconnect with our self, to become a *nefesh* again. If we are to climb hand-over-hand to reach up towards God, becoming human - allowing ourselves to feel and acknowledge our basic self - is where it all begins. We regain our *nefesh* as we learn to absorb the holiness of the Sabbath. We are told, commanded actually, that the *nefesh* needs fuel in order to continue to run well. The fuel of the *nefesh* is taking one day, withdrawing from the world in order to regain a healthy relationship with what is true. Setting aside time to be human and recapture awe is the sustaining force of the nefesh.

When we sit, pray, listen, learn, sing and are still, the world takes on brighter hues and restores the balance in ourselves once again. These are rejuvenating activities, not necessarily restful ones. Inhering in all that exists is holiness. Relating to life in a vital relationship to it, not as an observer, but as a participant, is what brings us back to our self.

Let's review: Life needs to be acknowledged. In the absence of conscious living we quickly become tired of a humdrum existence and seek meaningless distractions. We seek out new thrills. An ephemeral "high," however, is no replacement for simple awe. The *nefesh* desires to be nourished. Its needs are critical to our wellbeing and beg to be understood. If we wish to be part of the world, our *nefesh* must develop a relationship with everything. Some exercises to consider:

Smelling. Smell your food before eating it. Inhale the varied aromas that rise from the plate. Let those smells sink deep inside before partaking. After all, the smell is a part of the taste and experience of the food. Using the opposite as an illustration, when you have a cold, food had no taste. Eating is an act of simply staying nourished when we are not feeling well (which is why we often lose weight when we are sick). There is no joy in eating food and not being able to taste it. Therefore, the opposite of a having a cold is a heightened awareness of smell that will enhance the experience of the food.

Smell perfumes and colognes. Be aware of them. Be conscious of the many flavors that people sport.

Smell flowers. Like the proverb goes.....''take time to smell the roses.'' Literally. Stop. Smell not just the roses, though. Take a whiff of the plants. They each have a unique, if subtle, aroma.

Smelling allows us the opportunity to develop into a relationship with all that exists. That means acknowledging their existence which in turn makes our life so much richer. It is an act that feeds the nefesh.

Listening. There are many kinds of listening that are possible. What I refer to here is active listening. If a person is speaking, listen to them on as many levels as you can. For example, in hearing their words, listen to the passion that lies behind them. For this you will need to focus a lot of attention on their face, body language, tone, affect and much more. After developing a mature sense of this kind of active listening, you will probably know more about them in many ways than they know about themselves! Best of all, you have now entered into a relationship with them that is whole, not piecemeal. No longer will you just be listening to their words (which may be similar to listening to an opera without the orchestration) but to the depth of their being. Just sitting quietly and absorbing the multitude of sounds that are all around us can yield many benefits.

Looking. Watch life with your eyes. Take it all in. Every person you will ever meet has more to them than the biggest encyclopedia. Watch and absorb their talents and gifts. Also, the way a person will dress, speak and walk says volumes about their concerns and personality. The same goes for buildings. Each building has a design, a character, a nuance that is unique to it. We tend to notice buildings when we are in a distant land but take them for granted when we see them every day driving to work. Water, trees, bright signs all contribute to this rich tapestry waiting to be seen.

In truly looking at life we perceive so much more of the munificence of the world. Colors become more variegated and bright; foliage communicates with us; everything becomes a part of the mosaic of our life instead of a barrier to be surmounted or conquered.

Naturally, there is so much more to being awake than just these three items of smelling, listening and looking. Still, if we begin in these places the relational character of life will reawaken inside of us and energize our *nefesh*. We will begin to witness a personal rebirth, like Abraham and Jacob of long ago.

Chapter 11

Ruach

Humanity is blessed. Our intelligence and ability to search for more and deeper knowledge is certainly one of these great blessings. Our sense of inquiry and reason, induction and deduction, is to be celebrated because that gateway opens up so many other doors. Our next point of entry, or rung on the ladder, is that of *ruach*, the lynchpin, or gate to our higher senses.

Belonging to most religions in is the idea that reason must be used in all facets of our lives, including our faith. There have been some xenophobic, embattled eras of history, when intellect was viewed as the enemy of faith. Those historical footnotes are shameful episodes in our past.

Since humanity has been endowed with the gift of discernment, it would be a defilement of that present to allow it go unused. Reason is not the enemy of the soul; it is an endowment that adds immeasurably to our lives. There is a paradox, though. It would be a mistake to overestimate this God-given ability. Does our intelligence stand at the apogee of all our endowments? Kabbalah and other spiritual traditions tell us, no. As we discussed in the second chapter, it is misleading to believe that knowledge can cure all the spiritual needs of the soul. Ability to reason is *one* gift of many. Our reason is the springboard to the next level of spiritual growth. It is at once a gift and a vehicle.

Ruach, like the second son on Noah (Yafet, remember means *beauty*), adds a dimension of exponential depth, meaning and majesty to our lives. This aspect of our self is truly that which makes existence beautiful. Invariably, when we speak of spirituality we are talking about *ruach*. This beautiful or aesthetic quality of our self is what moves us to tears when watching a poignant scene in a movie, cry at a wedding or clap our hands in delight at a milestone of our daughter. When we see a painting which arrests our eyes or read a poem that translates itself into the unnamable parts of our being, our *ruach*'s voice is being heard.

A parable I heard many years ago tells of two religious pilgrims on a long journey. They pass days silently walking through dark forests and open, wide valleys. Murmuring prayers as they walked, the men shared meals, drank from mountain streams and passed the days in quiet contemplation. After a full week of walking, their silence was disturbed by cries coming from far below. They feverishly looked for the source of the cries and spied a body desperately flailing far below in a dangerous chasm. Without thinking, the two raced down the treacherous sides of the rock walls to rescue the person. Finally, the pilgrims reached a woman clinging for her life. Using all their energy the men hauled her up to safety.

Exhausted from her struggle with near-death, she whispered her weak thanks to the pilgrims. Then, taking turns, they hefted her onto their shoulders and carried the woman to the nearest village. They left the woman in capable hands to nurture her back to full strength.

Several hours later, the pilgrims were back on the road heading towards their original destination. They tried to return to their quiet reverie but one could not remain silent. He turned to the other and said, "You know, she was a beautiful woman. You did not have to carry her for such a long time. That was not proper for men of God like us."

Turning to his companion, he responded, "I put her down long ago. It is time you put her down too."

Ruach is attuned to beauty. Yet, like the two pilgrims in the tale, we can perceive beauty in different ways. Based on our *nefesh* (this is the first man who looks at the veneer of the woman and sees her as attractive) beauty is physical. So much of our life is consumed with listening to this voice. The advertising that we see, the movies that we watch, the radio that we hear, the magazines that we read are mostly directed toward this level. Based in our *ruach* (this is the second man who found beauty in the act of coming to the aid of the helpless) beauty is measured by an internal yardstick that looks at the beauty of life; not the outer shell. *Ruach* is accessing beauty with a higher level of the self.

That which distinguishes the former level, *nefesh* from *ruach* is that we take in all that the world offers but we process it through the filter of our senses, experiences and understanding. In short, *ruach* is where the conscious mind interprets what we have absorbed. The experience then rises well above the instinctual or animal level of life.

A different example to illustrate how the *ruach* works is a flower. One way the *ruach* would apprehend a rose is with the longer term memory of the flower. We can take the flower's smell and carry it away with us long after we left it. We have the ability to extend the experience of the rose by savoring its essence in our mind, seeing it in our imagination. In a way, we can change time by expanding it. We can also allow the sense of the flower to be felt emotionally, not just physically. We have the capacity to experience and enjoy the feeling of life flowing through it. There is a vital force that inheres in everything that exists, which we can share.

Our *ruach*, our spirit and breath, binds us to God. Remember that Creation came into being with breath and words. Earlier we discovered how the *ruach* floated above the primordial waters. What could this force be but the welling of the creative power about to form a universe? The gathering energy of the *ruach* is ultimately the force that wields the power to create. The Voice, which emerges from the *ruach*, of the Divine made the universe possible ("Let there be…"). The mixture of these two – Voice and spirit - was enough to bring about all existence.

Ruach is a special divine gift to humanity. Remember that God blew this force into the nostrils of the first being. Back then primordial man was merely a husk, a shell (or as Kabbalah calls it, a "shoe"). Once the breath of the Divine entered the husk, man was truly born. In this manner humanity was patterned or made in the image of God. Not that we look like God but we are the receptors of this *ruach*, breeze or spirit, which God infused into humanity. We were given the breath of God.

There are two unique aspects to the creation of mankind in the Bible. The first is from the earth. The body of the adam was culled from the soil of the ground. No other creature was so fashioned. For the balance of creation, God simply mentioned them and they came into existence. God thought "cow" and it came into being. Of man, God was like a potter who formed the elemental being from the ground and meticulously fashioned the arms, legs and torso.

That passage is deliberate to draw the reader's attention to the tactile nature of our inception. The mere thought of creation is not enough for man. Like the potter, God forms this being with His "hands." Our *nefesh* is the handiwork of God Second in the process of making the adam animate, was to breathe His *ruach* into the man. In two brief statements, the Bible indicates that the *nefesh* (the physical building of humanity) and *ruach* (the metaphysical component from God's "lips") are fundamental elements of humanity.

"And when Abraham, our father, may he rest in peace, gazed and saw and understood through his probings...creation came to him....[therefore God] stirred them with His breath."

--The Book of Creation

In this Kabbalistic work, "The Book of Creation," we are given a sense of Abraham's prescience; how he was able to peer at the world and see it, not just as it physically appeared to his eyes, but also to his higher sense. Abraham looked and saw life, every creation that litters the world, as pulsating with the vitality of God. For this patriarch, it was not just a world where he would agonize where his next meal might be coming from, or how to make the next barter more profitable or mapping out a strategy to go to war and capture more land and precious resources. Others perceived the universe in this way but Abraham's visions was far more expansive.

'Why was Abraham elected to be the forerunner of monotheism?' numerous Biblical commentators throughout the ages have questioned. Because he utilized both his *nefesh* and *ruach* Abraham was able to see far more than his contemporaries. He peered outward from his soul and witnessed the intense and deep beauty surrounding him. Abraham saw a world filled with sparks of God: a world that glittered with radiance to his eyes. That is why the Bible tells us that God stirred creation with his breath (*ruach*). It gently moved in every thing and person. That subtle, almost innocuous, act enabled the Divine essence to inhere in every creature. The holiness was planted long, long ago and waited in quiescence for one who would be born with the vision to recognize it. That someone was Abraham. Abraham saw it. It was there because Abraham knew it existed.

When we translate experience into words, thoughts and even abstraction, we alter and elevate the physical experience. The experience remains as it was. The exterior shell and the essence of the thing have not changed. With the gift of *ruach*, though, we have the ability to see higher levels of meaning in the ordinary. It was always present.

The key to spiritual awareness is understanding that there is more to life than that which meets the eyes. There is always more. In order to achieve the "more," the *ruach* must be acknowledged, accepted as genuine to absorb and integrate it into our self. This is how we begin to imitate God by taking the experience of the *nefesh*, fusing it with *ruach*, and elevating it to another level called creation. That is why *ruach* is likened to beauty; it is something we create that mimics our experience of it. It is our subjective, personal translation of the world and it is overflowing with beauty. And it portends coming closer to God.

Ruach is integration, a real knowing of the world. That is why later in the story of the creation of the second being, the Biblical text speaks of Adam and Havvah "knowing" one another. This "knowing", unlike the sexuality of animals, was a true and deep understanding and uniting of Adam and Havvah. The "knowing" that Genesis speaks of is much greater than just a physical familiarity. *Ruach* incorporates knowledge as a starting point but then goes well beyond it. It is a high state of awareness of the self and other.

Pinhas, the venerated teacher, used to say, "A person's soul will teach them." He added, "We are perpetually informed by our soul."

His pupil was confused and asked, "If that is the case, why do we have hatred and war? If the soul continually speaks, why are not all people good?"

"The soul will always enlighten and teach," replied Pinhas. "But it does not repeat itself."

Not that the spirit refuses to teach, Pinhas points out, but we effectively prevent it from doing so by willing the voice of the soul to an exile of silence. Its message appears only once for that moment. Afterwards, it is gone…

The dissonance of two conflicting voices of the Soul and the Self cannot be tolerated by most people. "Give it away," "share what you have" are voices on one side of the Self. "Hoard," "devise ways to get more," "giving things away means less for me," are some of the voices heard on the other side. When the soulful voice (*ruach*) rises and is contradicted by another more earthly voice, the soul voice often is shut down. We hear the voice of *ruach* is when we give permission for it to be heard. Shutting down that voice will mean the loss of the message. And, as Pinhas taught, it only comes once.

Listening to the soulful voice is not a typical "type A" personality. Being soulful, hearing the quiet voice of *ruach,* will contradict being the most aggressive salesperson. But I am not so sure that kind of lifestyle is truly human either. That is why Kabbalah stresses the importance of struggling to rise above the primitive level of the *nefesh*. Realization of the existence of the *ruach* is predicated on first coming to terms with and accepting the *nefesh*. To use a building metaphor, one does not pour the cement until the wooden borders are in place to hold the liquid cement. Likewise, the *ruach* is the natural second stage of acquiring holiness in our lives.

Idea: There is a beauty, bordering on luminescence, that inheres in the world. It is ever-present. Yet, as one poet of old said, "Beauty is in the eye of the beholder." Some people love pugs. Others shudder at them. Some people are drawn to the majesty of creatures of the sea; others deplore the very idea of them. We make up our minds about what we think is beautiful or ugly. Is it possible to see loveliness where we have not seen it before?

It is critical to be aware of beauty. In this stage of *ruach*, the **idea** of beauty is important. Since we determine what is beautiful and what is not, consider how different we would be if we were able to see beauty in more of life! Certainly the world would remain as it was, but our perception would dramatically change. The consuming radiance of the world is not confined to super models or ribbon-quality dogs. It is spread throughout the universe. There is beauty in everything.

The engine driving this higher state of living is the inward appreciation that every thing contains a spark of the Almighty. That spark is glorious. God inheres in all creation. Miracles abound. They lurk in the earth that nurtures plant life. It exists in the pebbles beneath our feet and the clouds above our heads. Why should we quake in awe only when confronted by a fierce storm, a double rainbow or magnificent rose? Why should humanity wait for a tsunami before feeling reverence for nature? Are we capable of feeling the awe all around us simply because we are part of this miraculous universe?

A review: The *nefesh* is an eye that is open to the world. It gazes out from its loneliness in the endless universe and positions itself physically. The *nefesh* stands with its feet against the earth, a bulwark against the wind and rain. This primary aspect of the self is the shell which envelopes, carries and protects the inner kernel, *ruach*-- the next and higher level of integration.

While a deep appreciation of the world is necessary and enhances our enjoyment of life, we can expand that dimension of joy by using our spirit, *ruach*, to connect with an ethereal universe. So much of what we see is colored by how we see it. The way in which we perceive the world is governed by how our minds apprehend that picture. Did you ever notice how some people see the ocean as a vast and calm place of refuge? Another person may be standing right next to the first and be enveloped by a feeling of emptiness as they stare out into the endless roll of blankness. It is simply stark and empty. To a diver, the ocean is a concealed playground of untold mystery. To yet another, the ocean is full of unknown terrors that lurk invisible and waiting just beneath the opaque surface. To all, they are gazing at the same ocean but their predisposition affects what they actually see.

There is an inherent beauty in all things-this we know from our life. There is a meta-beauty that can be perceived in all things as well. Like poetry, there is a rhythm and cadence to all things that exists, even if they are only ideas. *Ruach* takes the physical realm, moves it to a level of abstraction, and then offers to fill a vacant part of our soul with awe. The magnificence of the world is immeasurably heightened with the breath of life.

Tasks:
1. Summon up a vision of a person whom you know or whose face you are familiar with. Set that picture as a concrete image in

your mind's eye. Then utter a prayer to God on their behalf. Say a prayer for them with their physical form fixed in your head. Use the full power of that image along with the force of your prayer to appeal to God to listen.

Or take a flower, a bud or some natural growth and place it within eyesight. Rains will not dampen its enthusiastic growth as it will extend its tendrils into the air. Take your time in the process of visualizing the flow of energy between it and you; between you and it. Draw strength from that life. Gaze at it, focus on the minutiae of the plant and take acute notice of its quiet, yet insistent, power.

2. Focus on a holy place. From where you are now, bring your mind to the holiest place on earth and let it dwell there. When I conjure up an image of a holy place it is usually the Western Wall that sits in old city of Jerusalem. Massive stones poised on top of one and another rising hundreds of feet into the air. The stones are rough and smooth at the same time. They buffet and sooth the skin when you raise your hand to it. While ridges project outward from the chipped rock, they have been softened by the eons. Touched by people seeking a conduit to heaven, the Wall is a symbol of the connection that bridges heaven and earth. God is in this place.

Visualize your chosen place. Look at everything in your mind's eye. Be mindful of the texture of the surroundings, the sounds that would be present, the smells and colors and even the breeze blowing. The perceived reality of the mind is all that matters, so if the picture is askew in any way, or more to the point, if you feel that it is somehow not accurate, remember *reality is how we apprehend it*. All reality is subjective.

Chapter 12

Neshama

> An animal walks with its face to the earth, for earthiness and materiality is all that it knows. Man walks upright, for man was born to gaze upon and aspire to the Heavens."
>
> *-- DovBer of Mezritch*

The two tools needed for this next step are in hand. The *nefesh* and *ruach* enable us to make this next significant step of graduating to the level of the *neshama*, the highest point yet. Perched on the backs of *nefesh* and *ruach* we find this new level.

Much of what we have learned to this point may have a sense of familiarity about them. Learning about them may have provided a comfort; a warm recognition and affirmation of what we already knew. Perhaps you even found yourself nodding as you read some of those passages. That is good. Many people will have already arrived consciously to embrace these ideas.

Perhaps we merely intuited the existence of both those levels; perhaps we learned it through life's experiences. That, too, is good. Other parts of the past chapters may have been not so familiar. Perhaps they were tucked away more deeply. Where ultimate truth is concerned, even if it lies in the deep folds of your soul, there is nothing new that it did not know already.

"As we have heard, so we have seen," (Psalms 48:9). The voice that we have heard deep in our soul has a comforting resonance. In accessing the truth, we recognize it when we meet it. That is why it seems familiar to the point that we know have experienced it before. The ladder's next step upward is likewise already known to your soul. In fact, this next chapter will equip us to meet and become re-acquainted with an old friend. Lying shielded from our sight most of the time, the *neshama* is nonetheless ever-present, waiting and wanting for its voice to be heard and heeded. When we are adequately prepared by integrating *ruach* into our lives, we meet that which has existed inside of us --albeit, in a nascent form -- for our entire existence, *neshama*. It has been waiting for this moment.

First, the backdrop: "And the Lord God formed the adam [the earthen husk that would become the first man] from the earth and He blew *[ruach]* into his nostrils the soul *[neshama]* of life and the adam became a living being *[nefesh]*." *Genesis 2:7.*

We have already seen how the *nefesh* and *ruach* combine to form the body and animating force of humanity. Now, in this early passage from Genesis, the Bible is deliberate and clear about the three elements that God folded into our being. Using no extraneous words, the Text wants to tell us: "Look, this is what you are made from! If you want to know what makes you unique, humanity; allow your gaze to settle here. These three elements -- *nefesh, ruach* and *neshama* -- comprise the spiritual DNA of people." They are all specifically mentioned. While the English in the Bible misses the import of the union of these primary aspects of humanity, the Hebrew practically screams it out.

The details of the Hebrew version must not be glossed over: they are integral for our understanding of Creation. Like a code, the Bible deliberately uses three words to describe the formation of man. Unlike the creation of animal life, which the Bible dispenses with a single verb, humanity is crafted in three specified stages. Each stage is designed to show consecutively higher levels of potential.

At the Beginning, God created the first human in His image. What is God's *image*? Are we to imagine that God resembles Michelangelo's picture in the Sistine Chapel? Does he have a face? Hands? Do we really look like the Almighty? Are we cast to resemble Him with the same features? Does He have a voice and hair as we do? Of

146

course any anthropomorphic rendering of God is wrong-minded. If it were not true, we would have to invert the biblical idea to read: 'we have created God in our image,' instead of the other way around.

The holy Zohar teaches that the "image" that most resembles God is our *neshama*. This is how we look like God. Our spiritual essence, what ultimately connects human beings to Divinity, is what is called *neshama*. The ancient ones understood that we do not physically look like God. God cannot be reduced to such corporeal terms. But there is a segment of our being that does bear the image of God. Called the ultimate gift of God, this final element placed into the newly formed adam becomes the connective tissue between us and the Divine.

When a person is born, their innermost spiritual entity is given a vessel to house it: We call this vessel, the *nefesh*. It is a very primitive, unrefined house for the most exalted of gifts. It grazes and feeds. The *nefesh* struggles for survival by fighting to maintain its grip on life. With little regard for anything else, the *nefesh* exists for its own needs.

There is an old tale about a man made from mud in the medieval city of Prague. It is the original Frankenstein story. An earthen man, or "golem" as it was called, was a soulless creation of a great leader and Kabbalist. The Kabbalist gathered rich mud from the banks of the river that ran through Prague. Hidden in his attic, the famed scholar and mystic took the earth, pressed it into the form of a man. Then, using holy incantations and mystical versions of God's name, the golem opened its eyes.

The golem became an unthinking agent of his human creator. Simple instructions went awry as the golem fulfilled each of his missions, literally. Rampaging through the city of Prague, the golem had no moral sense enabling it to make appropriate choices. Instead of a good servant, the golem became a destroyer of life. The earthen being had no conscience, no *ruach* or *neshama*. Ultimately, the golem had to be destroyed. The story depicts what the *nefesh* would be like if it had no soul.

We, however, are not only created with *ruach* and a *neshama* but we are instructed to use them to attain a more meaningful life. With effort, we can rise above the animalistic self to attain --and utilize -- a sharper, more clear sense of life through the aspect of *ruach*.

Ruach takes the vapid earthen being and fills that vessel with joy, hope and infinite possibilities.

While the *nefesh* is most grounded in the physical, animal world and the *ruach* allows us to reach outward toward the unknown and unseen; the *neshama* extends far beyond the abilities of either level. Our *neshama* holds great, perhaps unlimited, potential for touching the Infinite and gathering its light. Once the *neshama* opens up its vault we feel enveloped by its great warmth. It feels like we have finally arrived.

The experience of feeling so embraced, safe and whole is not uncommon. Most people have had that feeling at least once in their life. It is a moment of clarity. It is when everything makes sense. In that timeless window, we understand why we exist. We know the purpose of life. All the usual demands of life become mere distractions that fade into insignificance. The conduit to heaven has opened. The purpose of this **Journey to the Soul** is to make the meeting not accidental, but intentional.

The richest, most meaningful, life is attained when we re-connect with this, the focal point, and beginning, of our existence. Should we rise to such a height of conscious awareness of our *neshama,* we will have realized the potential of what it means to be made "in the image of God." In this sense, we will then have become the "spark of the Creator clothed within a spark of the created." – *Tanya*

א א א א א

If a medicine works, prescribe it and use it. And what if we do not know why it works... but still it works? What should we do then? Prescribe it, use it and recommend it to others. That is my philosophy of life: If it works, use it.

I do not remember how many times throughout my years as a pulpit rabbi that parents approached me with the same internal angst. They came wanting to know why their child was disinterested in their faith. "How can I get them to come to services?", they would complain. "How do I get them to enroll in religious studies?" "How do I get them to care about their faith?" "Their heritage?"

Early on in my career (read: I was still green) I would offer to meet with the young person and talk them into trying to take an ac-

tive interest in their faith. It did not work. I thought I was being persuasive with my many arguments but when they left my office their
lives went back to the way they were before. Five minutes with me
in my office did nothing to change their mind. There was no argument that could advance, no smart or pithy line I could hand them
that had a lasting impact.

Through the years, though, I learned that there was something
that did make a difference to the young man or woman. I learned
from colleagues and parents who were far more insightful than I.
Experience was a great teacher. Later on in my career (read: no
longer so green), when a desperate parent would come into my office, I would reach down to a shelf beside my desk where I kept bro-
chures for Israel.

"Send them here," I would tell them, handing over one of the
glossy fold-overs. "You will drop them off at the airport. When
they come back you will meet someone transformed by an experience so profound that they will never be able to put it into words.
But you will know that it is real from the glow of their eyes. Do not
be surprised by the change."

I have not known it to fail. Visiting the Holy Land always has an
almost magical effect on travelers. If it works, use it.

I can only guess that when they see the land, as they experience
the vitality of the place; standing where Patriarch Abraham stood; it
is inevitable that some unknown, unnamed mystical spigot will be
turned on. A spiritual energy is then released. For the pilgrim of any
age that sensation triggers a transformation of character. For children, teenagers and adults visiting the ancient land is the start of accessing their soul. There, they touch something indefinable yet so
powerful it moves them in ways that will have a dramatic effect on
the rest of their lives.

What is the corollary mendicant for our life? What is the anti-
dote for assuaging the torn, fragmented and lonely person? What
works with the same unerring accuracy as the Holy Land? We know
that our soul yearns for something which will bring a sense of com-
pleteness. We are creatures in search of healing. Where is the cure
for what ails us?

When we finally grab hold of our *neshama*; when we supply
what the heart has been pining for all our years, we experience an in-

tense and meaningful change. The touchstone of our lives is the moment when we meet us. That introduction takes place when we allow our *neshama's* voice to speak. The aftermath of connecting with the *neshama* is the taste of wholeness.

א א א א א

We speak to God on many different levels. The language of humanity takes many forms. At each one of these levels our voice can be heard. But, from the other direction, the language of God is understood by the *neshama*. True dialogue with the Infinite One happens at this level. *Neshama* transcends the physical realm; it rises to a place where there is no human speech. In the realm of the *neshama*, no words are necessary; they are simply not adequate.

An advisory: The arrival at this highest point of *devekute*, cleaving to God, is predicated on our grasp and ascent of three prior rungs.

We must adhere to the "deep desire to lead and live a good, pure life" as a prerequisite to traveling the path of reclaiming our *neshama*. How we behave is important but now our desire, or intent, plays an integral role. Having said this now a second time, *intent* plays a very important role in fixing our inner eye on the *neshama*. Accessing the highest part of our self requires desire. In the physical universe, what we do matters most of all. In the arena of the Kabbalah, intent is critical. It is not simply what we do, but the narrow and fixed shaft of unwavering intent that is the driving force behind the deed.

Can one hope to cleave to God while crushing the spirit or standing on the bodies of the Holy One's other creations? The spiritual journey of the nexus is direct but does not exist in a vacuum. The ladder has a series of calibrated steps before this one.
1. The deep desire to lead and live a good, pure life. We may not always succeed but we must never stop trying to refine our self through our intentions and actions.
2. The reaching of the two prior steps of understanding the *nefesh* and integrating the *ruach* is the internal litmus test that you have successfully rekindled them inside and then
3. The joining of both *nefesh* and *ruach* into a seamless whole before proceeding to accept the *neshama* as the cord that binds us to God.

א א א א א

A teaching: "A sigh can break a person's body." Rebbe Nachman explains that when words fail, when all our prayers have been exhausted; what remains behind? A sigh can breach the barrier to our *neshama*. The sigh transcends the limitations of the *nefesh*. The language of the soul is not limited to words. In fact, sometimes we are constrained by them. Yet, a single sigh can shatter the boundaries of the body and allow our soul to speak and be heard.

In Exodus, the story of the enslavement is told. Beaten and deprived of humanity, the Pharaoh afflicts the nation. In an attempt to annihilate them, the Pharaoh ruthlessly attacks and murders this people. All the cries of the Children of Israel, all the pleas for release, the relentless lashes of the masters, the screaming and tormented howls went unanswered. For hundreds of years, the tormented heard only silence.

The story then states, "It came to pass in the days when the Pharaoh died that the Children of Israel *sighed* because of their bondage…."

Then the ears of God listen. Only when the Children of Israel sigh are their prayers carried to heaven. Only then does redemption begin its course.

A tale: A long time ago lived a shoemaker, poor and pious. The shoemaker would rise early each day to attend to his work. People brought their worn shoes to him, which kept him very busy but not well-paid. The shoemaker eked out a meager living that barely put food on his table and clothes on the backs of his children. He complained bitterly to his rabbi, "I have no time to spend with God. I work from early morning until night and spend every last penny on the needs of my family. Never do I stop worrying where the next meal will come from… or what would happen to my children if I would die. When? When will I finally have time to pray to God?" Deeply the shoemaker sighed as he bared his heart.

"That man's sigh," the rabbi told his students later, "was the holiest prayer I have ever heard. It could have broken the doors to heaven."

A lesson: Sometimes the opening of the innermost parts of the soul happens when we let down our barriers.

Intent

In the above shoemaker illustration, the sigh becomes the powerful vehicle to connect with God. In the physical world, a sigh is meaningless. It does not change the world. It does not feed the hungry or perform any of the commandments outlined in the Biblical or extra-biblical texts. And yet it is the ultimate prayer. On the back of our deeds and desires—not our accomplishments --- stands a most valuable treasure. In accessing our *neshama,* the purposefulness behind our actions becomes the force that propels our soul to reveal itself.

Too live a good life *and* feel the vibrations of the *neshama* is a purposeful venture. It does not just happen. Like the mundane activity of walking, being good can also become an unconscious motion. We learn to do the right thing by repeating identical or similar actions. Placing one foot in front on the other. A good person will act out of goodness as a reflex action. It is performed unthinking. This is the definition of a good human being: One who immediately responds to another being's needs without dwelling on what they might lose in the process. There is no inner conflict when they see an out-stretched palm.

Our minds already know what is good: We know that giving to those who have empty pockets is good. It does not have to be taught and re-taught. We know that helping a person find their parked car in a sea of vehicles is good. We know that providing someone with directions, helping them fix a flat tire, giving a kind word or sharing our lunch is all good. Here is a key idea: At the *neshama* level, we no longer perform these acts through repetition. Instead, the spiritually aware person opens the inner recesses of their heart to be aware of every action, ever conscious of these same deeds as a way of pleasing God. Such consciousness feeds our *neshama.* This is where intent becomes the most powerful tool of the soul as well as the sustenance of the *neshama.*

So that we do not erect self-limiting roadblocks on our path, it is good to prime ourselves with a few questions:

- How much do you want to access and feel the Holy One? Do you wish to be touched by God? Understanding that the goal of enlightenment is consistent with yearning to connect with the Holy One is a sine qua non. The response to this question will ultimately determine our success at accessing the *neshama*.

- Does this desire extend to the deepest part of your self? Or is the internal path leading to that relationship blocked by fear or indecisiveness? You already know, but let it be stated nonetheless, that connecting with the Holy One will filter through to all aspects of the self and affect the rest of our lives. Are you ready?

- "What if God actually hears me?" must not be the question which motivates all students of the Kabbalah. Instead, the heartfelt sigh that reaches upward is the goal. That is the language of God.

One of the most important characteristics of the *neshama* is love. Love is commanded in many biblical statements that are scattered throughout the Holy Text. But can love be commandeered by a person? Or even by God? How can you control or command love? Is a legitimate path to love to say to someone, "Now you must love me."? Can such a relationship really work? Of course it is absurd. Such depth of emotion does not happen that way.

A commanded love is not love. If love for another person cannot be demanded, how much more can love for God, whom we cannot fathom let alone the fact that He goes unseen, not be expected? Even though we are explicitly told to "love God with all your heart..." in the Bible, the Sages understood this was fundamentally not possible. Love can only come from a willing, open heart; one that desires God.

The *only* tool of the soul is love. In fact, Kabbalah goes further to share with us that attachment or yearning for God is the soul's raison d'etre, its total reason for existence. The whole reason for having a soul is to love. This is what the *neshama* does. It acts as our vehicle to reunite with the Source of everything. The *neshama* is our sole linkage to God. It is the way through which we can find and express the love that the Bible speaks of.

Love for God, described by prophets and Kabbalists, is sometimes called 'ecstatic love.' Unlike an earthly love which may be predicated on physical attraction or mutual need, there is no other way to label the kind of love that has no ulterior purpose than *devekute*. Love for love's sake. That is all. It is an ecstatic, joyful love having its root in wanting the *neshama* to be in connection with the Great Well from which it was initially drawn. Ecstatic love, the kind of joy which cannot be bounded, emerges once the *neshama* has

freed itself from the limiting factors and ideas that have been empha-
sized and labeled as earthly love. It is limitless.

The religious word we tend to use describing this kind of love is
prayer. Surprised? Prayer, at its fundamental core, is nothing more
than a poem of love. Are King David's Psalms really that much different from Browning's poems? They are deeply emotional testimonies to love. The major difference between them is King David's
object of love, God. The pathway of relating to God is through this
tried medium with a slight difference....

"Whoever serves God out of love," says the *Zohar*, "comes into
union with the place of the Highest of the High and comes into union
with the holiness of a world yet-to-come".

א א א א א

In an opaque medieval text called the "Book of the Formation of
the Embryo," the idea of a pre-birth of existence raised. The manu-
script questions whether the moment of birth is the same as the moment when our soul came into being. Our soul was not conceived
along with our body, the book declares. The soul came into being
well before our birth. The text has dramatic implications.

The "Formation of the Embryo" begins by considering the function of Angels. One primary task of Angels, the book indicates, is to
reveal to all souls the place of their birth and moment of their death.
The chosen messenger (the term 'Angel' means *messenger*) informs
and escorts each soul through the travels it will soon undertake. Everything, including the moment when it will be ensconced into its
newly formed body, is shown to the soul. After revealing to these
ethereal souls the unique pathway which will take them through their
physical life, showing them various sites and events yet-to-be; it is
then the responsibility of the Angel to take this all-knowing soul and
place it within the womb of its mother.

After full gestation, the Angel appears a second time to the soul.
This time the Angel touches the physical form of the child, not just
the soul. As that happens, the light above the head of the fully
formed baby is extinguished. In an instant, it forgets all that it once
knew. Then, frightened and shorn of its knowledge, the baby
emerges into this world crying, bereft at the now distant and quickly

dimming memory of the universe.

This story, accounting for the cleft just beneath the nose, also indicates that the soul possesses a great understanding which lies dormant, just under the skein of consciousness, ready to be woken. The soul, if given opportunity to speak and be heard, will recognize and rekindle the desire to be close to holiness, God. Love and attachment (*devekute*) is the active part of reclaiming the voice of the soul.

The yearnings, the pull of the *neshama*, takes forms, like:

"Is this all there is to life?"

"Why does success mean so little to me? Why doesn't it fill me?"

"Why can't I just be content with what I have?"

The questions are different ways that the soul expresses itself. And all the wrenching questions mean the same thing; the soul is crying to be acknowledged, heard and nourished.

"In one of the most exalted parts of heaven, there is a palace called the Palace of Love... there are gathered all the most beloved souls of the Heavenly King; the Holy One blessed be He, lives with these holy souls and unites with them in love." (Zohar) The goal of the *neshama* and the peak of its ultimate wish is to revisit this palace. Inasmuch as the journey of the soul began with an Angel holding the keys revealing everything, so the soul desires to regain that sense of totality and wholeness for itself. The *neshama* knows what it needs.

There are different ways to approach the *neshama* and insure that there remains an ongoing dialogue with it. Many are so old that they encroach on the borders of recorded time. Yet among the two most important stages on the journey to reclaim the soul are

1. The ongoing nurturing of the *ruach* and *nefesh* and
2. The longing to become a whole, unbroken self.

In the first instance, the well can go dry unless the supply is replenished. If these two lower levels are neglected, the stepping stone to the *neshama* will be beyond our reach. It cannot be achieved without the first owning lower rungs. If the basement (nefesh) and walls (ruach) of the structure are compromised, the roof (*neshama*) will not be able to stand. This is an important idea as Kabbalah does not ask us to scourge the body or abnegate the self in order to reach into the soul. Instead of wearing hair shirts and immersing in cold baths, God implanted in us the *nefesh* and *ruach* to act as guide rails on our ascent.

155

Jonathan M. Case

Being attentive to the song of ruach and nefesh is therefore critical to the maintenance of a relationship with the *neshama*.

The second issue, desire, the want to connect with God, is also critical to recognize. Ascent will not happen of its own accord; we must want to access the highest soul.

"The king is dead. Long live the king." The meaning of the common saying is that a section of us must give way to make room for the new presence, the new king. Once the old habits and temporal goals have been set aside for what is meaningful and genuine, we say that the old rules (the old king) is now dead. The new monarch can then take its rightful place.

It is doubtful that we will be the same person we used to be once we have developed a living, breathing relationship with our soul. The things that mattered before to us will not count for so much any more. Other things will matter much more. Would it be surprising to learn that working overtime does not seem to hold the same reward as we felt before? Will others sense something significantly different in the way we deal with them? Will our lifestyle alter its previous course? The answer to all these questions and every other one that is like it is, of course, yes.

caveat

Change is not easy. Realizing, on a visceral level, that genuine transformation takes effort at the outset is wise. In this way we can articulate to the people we love, how we are striving to be different and attempting to embrace an internal change. This communication is an act of caring and love. It prevents misunderstandings when they see us behaving in a way that is unfamiliar to them. In addition, when we see people changing their behavior we tend to become frightened. We do not know what this change means for us, or them. Others will probably have the same reaction.

One of the most disturbing issues that I have had to deal with as a clergyman throughout my career is when children decide to make good choices about their life…that significantly differ from the way their parents have lived. For example, a young man who spent time abroad and returned home, wanted to be more observant and reli-

156

gious. He came to talk with me.

His parents, frantic and in deep pain, were also anxious for me to talk to young Robert - then in his early twenties- out of praying every morning. He needed quiet when he prayed. The rest of his family did not know what to make of Robert so they all tiptoed around every morning when he began his intonations. They were fearful that dinners would be compromised by his piety. "He says prayers all the time," they complained. The family did not know how to cope with Robert's new lifestyle. They were confused and a little scared.

"It's not like we don't respect what he is doing..." began the father.

"But it so weird having this different person in our home," continued the mother. "It's like having a stranger come in. I do not even recognize Robert any more. He looks at us weirdly when we do not go with him to services. He needs to have someone speak to him some common sense. The world just isn't like this! He has to grow up. This is a world where it is 'dog-eat dog' and he will never survive like this. Rabbi, you have to talk some sense into him."

Now, this might sound like a bizarre issue to bring to clergy (after all, what is the clergyman supposed to answer? Isn't that terrible? Praying all the time? Tsk. Tsk. We'll have to do something about this!) but it was forthright and honest of Robert's parents to bring this problem to me. After all, society generally does not think well of people with such religious proclivities. We reward people for obvious status conquests like buying a new condominium or luxury automobile, not for attaining higher levels of prayer. In countless variations I have had this issue brought before me throughout my career. I suspect all clergy have encountered the same conundrum.

So, here is the warning: Changing yourself will have an effect on people around you. It will. Odds are that people will not welcome the change either because it is unknown and therefore frightening. Tell them what you are going through or trying to attain. Expect resistance. Remember: People do not like change, especially when it concerns people they care about. It feels dangerous to them because they do not know what to expect.

Everyone has the same basic needs. We like to know what to expect when we enter a room. It gives us power and comfort. Not knowing what is going to happen may be alright for a circus but at least we know we can leave a circus if we do not like the show. It is not so simple with relationships. We cannot just walk out. If knowing what to expect empowers us, not knowing must dis-empower us, and for many people that can be terrifying.

A brief review:

Rabbi Simon was the founder of Kabbalah roughly two thousand years ago. Once he went on a journey with Eleazar, his son. He said to Eleazar, "It is astonishing to me that people give so little consideration to the study of the secrets of a soul's life and the good law. Do you remember what Isaiah said? 'My soul delights in You during the night. My spirit seeks You early (27: 9).' Simon then continued, "When we fall asleep at night, our soul leaves the body and ascends. So do all souls. They ascend and behold the face of the king."

Like Dorothy having arrived at the mythic source of Oz realized, the power has been there all along. It dwells inside. That which society impresses upon us from the beginning of our lives inches us away from the source of all; but the soul remains within. Sometimes quiescent and perhaps dormant, the soul nonetheless is present. Waiting.

However much we have been led, or have chosen, to ignore the voice of the soul, it is still there. Its voice may sometimes grow insistent; other times barely audible but it has been with us from before the beginning of life. To access that inner life with a full heart, all we need do is seek out with absolute love one's self and God. That alone is the requisite for reclaiming the *neshama*. The beating heart of this connection is desire, *devekute*.

Idea: Start with calling out God's name when you are ready. Begin in the quiet of your safe place by mentioning the holy Name over and over. Sometimes beginning is as simple as this.

Remember the admonition: Love demands that we inform others of the journey that we are on. It is important to tell them we will not stop loving them and, at the same time, ask them to keep in mind that this is a moment of growth for us. They do not need to accompany us on the journey. We only ask that they respect our heart's journey.

Section Two: A Practicum

Fresh from insight gained from the first section of this book, we draw upon that knowledge and wield it for the sake of growth. Those same principles will be applied towards the task of crafting a different world view.

> *The human mind is not capable of grasping the Universe. We are like a little child entering a huge library. The walls are covered to the ceilings with books in many different tongues. The child knows that someone must have written these books. It does not know who or how. It does not understand the languages in which they are written. But the child notes a definite plan in the arrangement of the books - a mysterious order which it does not comprehend, but only dimly suspects.*
>
> *-- Albert Einstein*

Chapter 1

Checklist for life

Is a book merely a book? Or does it indicate something greater? For one, a book implies that it has an author. Books do not write themselves. Even if the cover does not indicate the writer's name, we know that someone took the effort to create the book. A book is an indicator of a mind; it is not a random act of nature.

For two, can the existence of the book trigger a moment of quiet awe or appreciation for the hundreds of large and tiny steps necessary for before the pages were finally glued into their binding? A book represents a long chain of processes that began from a kernel of an idea; to writing and editing; to printing and distributing. There are many steps from the point of creation to the moment of holding a book in your hands. It was written, edited, proof-read, designed, printed, bound and carted so that it could be purchased at a store.

For three, the presence of a book in a room shows that *someone* purchased it, kept it, placed it on the shelf. A person wanted that book. It did not arrive there of its own volition. A book is far more than some wood pulp with ink randomly sprayed on it. It has a long pedigree.

A book is a symbol of much thought, deep consideration, creativity and hard work by many people. Just the fact of the existence of the book can inspire gratitude and a sense of wonder. That is why if we experience the awe when holding a book, then that volume has become a symbol, or metaphor, for something much larger.

The line of logic would go on to say that everything is a symbol or metaphor for/of something else. Consider a single strand of grass. Its ubiquitous nature makes that blade virtually unnoticeable. Since it is everywhere, why would our eyes linger over one? Why should we pay attention to it? What do we see when we look at grass, if we see it at all?

If the grass can be seen through the prism of a metaphor, what would it say? Like books, does a thoughtful consideration of grass bring any awareness into our field of consciousness? Should grass mean anything to us? That small life might provide an insight into humanity, an understanding of how we can touch God.

An Observation: Tiny, innocuous, green and often overlooked, grass abounds in every conceivable place. It sprouts in the fissures of the median strip along the streets we travel. It grows in the small fractures of pavement on the sidewalk. It is the cause of much energy output from weedwhackers and lawnmowers. Grass is often an annoyance because of its resilience in the face of technology and resistance to weed killer. Throughout the long summer months, homeowners and laborers constantly work to get the grass growth under control. Indefatigable, they are outside hacking away, mowing, spraying and fertilizing these shoots.

Besides occupying much of our time, energy and money, grass also provides hue and patina to a whirling palette of variegated colors. Grass is like the canvas backdrop of a painting. Without grass the physical view would be blah, empty. Imagine a stark white canvas with a portrait drawn upon it. Behind the portrait, the rest of the picture remains against rough, unpainted background. How would that look to you? Would you buy it? Chances are, people would look at it and wonder what happened to the artist. "Did he die before he had the chance to finish his work?" they might ask.

Think of a meadow with no splashes of green. Imagine a garden with an assortment of varied shades of color, but no finely trimmed lawn around it. What about a house surrounded by dry, brown dirt? How appealing is that? There is more.

A Commentary: A green, perfectly manicured, lawn does not appear in nature as an uninterrupted flow, does it? The lawn signifies many things. For one, green turf does not happen. It needs seeds, water and light. Lawns are drawn from the earth by first placing seeds on fertile, blank soil. Once settled on the dirt, still nothing will happen; those seeds will not mature and grow unless its shoots are first nourished by the sun and water. The sun will provide enough energy for the grass to grow. That is still not sufficient for the seedlings to dispatch roots down in search of a hold within the earth's mantle. Without enough rainfall or adequate natural water supply, people will have to do the work of bringing water to the seeds to ensure the grass' life.

Second, grass is a sign that there is an owner who has taken deliberate time to plant, and afterwards to fertilize and weed. It is no small task to craft an attractive lawn. One must carefully edge the borders of the grass so that the lines are defined and symmetrical. In addition, weeds have ample opportunity to send their implacable shoots down into the soil despoiling the perfection. Those lovely springtime dandelions are the bane of landowner's efforts. Like an abscess, they draw the life-blood out of the soil making it impossible for the grass to remain. Absence of weeds is a certain sign that diligence has been focused on this patch of land.

Grass growing unimpeded, not struggling for survival against the strong and numerous strains of weeds, to reach its richest green is not automatic. If the watcher of the soil, guardian of the plot, is nowhere in sight, the tell-tale signs of the insidious and incessant growth of the weeds will begin to scratch away at the lawn. It will soon be overrun. A well-tended lawn is therefore an indication of a mindful presence and artistry. The grass is a symbol of someone's attentiveness. Even if we actually never observe a person fertilizing the lawn or mowing, it is implicit that there is a guardian. Watchful care is not far removed from the verdant beauty. Something so linear could not happen in nature by itself.

Primary Interpretation: The symbol of grass is a correlate to God's existence. Such order does not just happen randomly. Just as an unperceived force draws the grass upward toward a deliberate life pattern with few weeds, defined borders, clipped edges, verdant green color, so too it is inconceivable that the world could exist without a Master. We may not see the gardener but it takes no great leap of imagination to know that there is a mind behind the perfectly clipped blades of grass. Someone, we understand, is the caretaker of these grounds. A Force is responsible for the larger garden too, the one we call the universe.

A Commentary: We may plant seeds but we do not create these embryonic pods of possibility. If a person has a well-tended lawn, they will feel proud of the beauty they mastered. All the careful planting, watering, choice of seed, watchful monitoring for the intrusion of alien growth is an ode to the artist.

Looking at steps that are far removed from the landscape artist laboring in the garden, we find the engineer who designed the machinery possible for the shifting of water from a far away lake to the garden hose. An engineer designed machinery to filter the water and pumps to send the water shuttling through miles of pipeline wending their way to our spigot. Without the successful work of those engineers, no grass would ever crack the earth's crust forming lush green patterns around our homes. Of course, the landowner purchased the grass seed from a vendor. That vendor, in its turn, purchased a hybrid designer seed culled from strains of grass known to thrive in certain environments; shade, wet, arid, hot, cold....

And the seeds? Where do they come from? Are they specially crafted from the start in a laboratory? These seeds are part of the organic industry called nature. No person can create them. All people can do is experiment with what only can nature provide. People may till the soil, plant grass seeds in the ground, water the soil and pull weeds that choke the new sprouts but they only *manage* what God has cast.

We may plant seeds but we do not create them.

Secondary Interpretation: Grass is a natural growth that generates and regenerates. For those who live in the far north, grass dulls in the fall until it becomes a lifeless brown in wintertime. Then, come spring, the grass' life-force propels it into a stage of rapid growth, recouping its now awakened luxuriant texture. It rises from its winter dormancy and is flush with life once more. Can grass be a metaphor for a life after death? Could it be a metaphor for the body's immeasurable healing power?

A Commentary: Seeing something for more than it appears, is uniquely spiritual. Such vision transforms the ordinary into the sublime. In this second interpretation, we veer towards a Kabbalistic mindset. Grass becomes a symbol of a power that transcends life. Grass will not be ordered by the natural cycles of life and death that we see animals experience. Rabbits, cats, polar bears and humans are born and die. They come into existence and then disappear forever. Grass knows no such boundaries.

While our eyes perceive only life, death and then a renewal of the cycle with new birth, grass offers us a new metaphor for understanding death. It falls into a winter slumber that appears like death. That death is an illusion as the grass will be reborn in the spring. Perhaps the lesson drawn from our observation of grass is that if our vision were expansive enough, we would see that death is as impermanent as life. It might be that there is much more to existence than we would otherwise learn from sight.

One of the basic premises of Kabbalah is that nothing is all that it appears. There is so much more to be gleaned from our experiences with life. A not-so-hypothetical question to ponder: What if the information in the last commentary is correct? What if death is simply the next chapter or step of life?

In one ancient text, some two thousand years old, Rabbi Jacob remarks, "This world is a foyer leading to the next." A foyer is only a passageway; a route to something much larger and greater. Not only is there a universe that exists beyond this one, the sage indicates, but it is more meaningful, more vital than the universe we inhabit. What we see is only the point of entry. Is this true? Can it be so?

If Rabbi Jacob's statement was accurate, how would this knowledge change our perception of death? If Rabbi Jacob is correct then we would also have to answer how this knowledge would impact our understanding of life. If this is so, how would we change the way we live? Would death be as terrifying and painful knowing that some far grander universe lay on the other side of life? Would life be more, or less, tolerable? And, how would this expanded view of a three dimensional universe change the way we look at things today?

Everything is at once real and a metaphor. It is real because we live in this place. Grass grows, requires fertilization and needs to be cut. This is our physical space; the one that dominates our waking hours. And yet life is also a metaphor waiting to be unraveled. Grass also carries a message that it wants to deliver to the *neshama*, soul; a message of life and rebirth. It is a power-laden metaphor that indicates there is more to the cosmos than our eyes see.

The next few chapters are devoted to developing a new perspective from the usual eat, drink, work, and sleep cycle. It is as we have long suspected: There is something far grander than mere survival. Every thing, event and person is generally viewed by us monochromatically. That is to say, we only see one single facet or dimension of people, places and things. We see this most clearly when we look at ourselves through another person's eyes. Some people look at us and see an academic; someone both studious and learned. Others view us as industrious and creative. Still others opine that we are stupid and foolish. How can all of them be true simultaneously? They are based on their observations of us and from their vantage, this is who we are. Since they contradict one another we say that one or more of them are based on misperceptions. They are wrong. They cannot all be correct.

A more accurate picture of us, and understanding of them, is that we meet all these descriptions and then more. At times, we have been stupid or foolish. At other moments we have been wise and a good advisor. We are very complex beings and are able to show many different facets of ourselves at various times. We are kind and stingy. We are healers and destroyers. Now, if this is true of us, must it not also apply to others? Aren't they *more* than how we have labeled them, i.e. limited, them?

Listen. Chandra is a nurse. She has worked in the same Nursing Home for several years. She does her job well bringing a positive attitude to what are often very frustrating situations. Daily, dressing the part with her white outfit, she travels to work where the needy anxiously await.

Estelle is one of Chandra's patients. She has been in the Home for at about two years. Estelle has a daughter who lives nearby by but she does not visit her mom very often. Chandra has sympathy for Estelle's daughter as she recently confided, "This is one tough woman, Estelle. She is a chronic complainer. None of the nurses like dealing with her. Like an angry dog, Estelle latches on to whatever is bothering her and growls, barks and howls until everyone around her is miserable. She even chased out her latest roommate. Estelle made life so miserable for Rhonda that the poor woman demanded to be taken out of the room shared with Estelle after just two days!"

One of the ongoing complaints that Chandra heard was the insistence that Estelle be given needles and thread so that she could sew her clothes. Chandra, the obliging nurse, has a motto: "Since these people are mostly here in a bad situation, I see my job as trying to give them things to make them happier. More settled."

So Chandra regularly did her best to find needles and thread and then put the tiny thread through the infinitesimal sized eye. Although it took energy and time from her rounds with the other patients, not to mention time away from other needy people, Chandra did this at least once a week.

"None of the other nurses want anything to do with her because Estelle is never happy. She is a pain," said Chandra. "All she ever does is complain and yell at the staff day and night."

One day Chandra was going through some items at home and found a small sewing kit she had picked up somewhere in her travels. The next day Chandra brought it in and gave it to Estelle saying, "Here, Miss Estelle, look what I have for you. It is a small pack of needles and thread. And guess what? The needles are all threaded! You can do it all yourself."

She was silent. Estelle's eyes grew moist. She turned to this nurse and said softly, "Thank you for the needles and thread, Miss Chandra. But what really makes me happy, the reason I am crying, is because you remembered me. You thought of me when you were not here."

Estelle did not change. She is the same today as she was back then; crotchety, bitter and demanding. What has changed is Chandra and her larger understanding of the patient. No longer is this nurse dazed and annoyed about her patient. Chandra knows exactly what Estelle needs to feel whole. She has empathy for Estelle. As a result, Estelle feels good whenever Chandra is her charge nurse and Chandra has an expanded view of Estelle which makes her more tolerant, less angry and more able to care for her patients, all of them, without feeling 'burned' by Estelle's many demands.

Idea: Kabbalah begins with a deep interior look and a realistic view of who we are while making ongoing assessments and reassessments of our potential. That is why we started this journey with defining who we are. In almost every instance, we are greater, endowed with more untapped potential, than we believed. Only when we have accomplished that goal, when we have grappled with 'who we might really be' under all the labels and window dressing -- or at least accept that our life has been self-limiting--- can we begin to move outward to see what lies just beyond what we thought was the extent of our reach.

There are two worlds for each human being: One is the inner world and the other is the one that which exists outside of our self. Our inner world informs the texture and hues of the multicolored threads of life. It is akin to the eye which perceives depth and color. With the information gained by the sweep of our vision, the mind then interprets all that data and forms an opinion about what we have seen. Our vision, what we see, is subjective. To employ biblical imagery, we create life in our own image.

What power! To craft a whole universe bound to the way in which we have chosen to construct it. We interpret what we see and, therefore, are ever in the act of creating it. We are the builders of our reality.

The essence of change begins with this idea: If we possessed enough strength to release the pre-judged (prejudiced) information that we hold, it might then be possible to discover another universe beyond. The freedom to be unfettered from judgment allows people and the rest of creation to reinvent itself unhindered by our interference. This is a source of great power as it enables us to see the world with a new urgency, a world just born, ripe for discovery. All we have to do is open our hearts.

Suddenly we loom larger and are filled with endless possibility; more than we thought, irreplaceable to God and the cosmos. In this vessel that we call the human body we are capable of all things: killing and healing, planting and desecrating, sharing and hoarding. Our consciousness elects, or chooses, the path we wish to take. The strength of the mind bears the resources necessary to break free of the cords inhibiting our growth. We choose the road we walk on. All it takes to make a different choice is a new perspective, one not jaundiced by narrow-mindedness. At the same time that we recognize our own potential, we also become aware that every other person is far grander than we, and even they, know. Every human being is an ever-evolving person. Yet, these two micro-universes are interconnected. One will affect the other.

We have learned: Our vision is myopic. Our minds limit what we can see. Like the flyspeck on the Monet canvas, all we see is the fly-speck and ignore the great artist's magnificent painting. In order to see the whole picture and not just a fragment, we need to allow our minds greater access to absorb the whole. There is more. There is al-ways more. Just as we learned with grass, there are an infinite number of ways to observe and relate to everything. Taken this way, all of life becomes a potential instructor of how to live a meaningful life.

Task: Take time to breathe. As we learned earlier in chapter 7, humanity was created with the Divine breath. So too, being aware of that animating force in the universe, con-scious breath has the ability to link ourselves with the spirit of God. More than becoming aware of the ruach, breath of life, try to breathe in the world. Take time during the day to not just be conscious of that spirit but also breathe in the spirit of other forces in the world.

Consider grass. It is a good and elemental place to begin. All things are part of the connective tissue that leads to God, including grass. Grass is a great instructor, like all things. The Talmud shares an insight: "Each day an Angel whispers to a blade of grass, "Grow, grow." In its own understated unique way the ancient ones were telling us there are great mysteries and revelations that inhere in the smallest, most in-nocuous things in the world.

Do not confuse nature with God, but understand that all creation contains shards of the Holy One. Allot some minutes that will not be lost in your day and focus on the grass as a means of approaching God. Breathe in the scent of the fauna. Observe it closely and allow its gentle dance in the breeze to speak to your innermost self. A plant next to your desk or even an inert piece of paper can accomplish the same end.

Others may limit us by their prejudices. When they believe that we are dumb, our ability to be "smart" in their presence and perhaps lasting well beyond that time (long after we have left and even some-times after they have departed) is diminished. Whatever opinions others hold of us will limit our capabilities in their eyes and perhaps even more insidious, in our eyes. If someone comes to a person with an uninformed or informed opinion, it is limiting. It does not matter whether what they think is grounded in reality; something they have observed, heard from someone or based on the way we look. Either way, it is a prejudice and limiting.

As previously said, if all individuals have a greater potential and ability than they reveal at any time, then it follows that a preconception, even if it is based on observation, is a wrongful preconception. After all, how do we know what we see is true? Can we be sure that it is never changing?

Thought: Even if the original assessment was correct, can a person find the inner resources to change? Can that change be thwarted with a single word? Is it possible that with our preconceived notion we can push them back from the brink of a dramatic personal change? Especially if it spoken by someone who cares? If this is true for how others see us, it must also be true for how we see and limit them.

But let's be selfish for a moment: If we can free ourselves from limiting their potential because of our prejudice, we will not only help them develop and grow... it will also free us from carrying an undue burden that often transforms itself into hostility. Isn't that reason enough to grant a person our mindful ability to let them be who they are at that moment?

Task: Play a game. Let's call the game, "The First Time." For every person that you come into contact with for the next say, four hours, treat them like you are meeting them for the first time. While it is obviously impossible to totally wipe out everything we know about them, try hard to form opinions about them based only on what they say and how they behave now. Doubtless, we will see formations of their character that we might otherwise have ignored or not have been able to see. The game might be a real eye-opener. And, what a blessing it would be to play this game for the rest of your life!

Chapter 2

Getting Up

> "And you who cling to the Lord, your God, are alive, totally, to-day."
>
> *--Deuteronomy, 4:4*
>
> "The world is delicately balanced between those who bring goodness and life to the world and those who bring evil and death to it. A moment will come when that righteous balance will be so measured that one person could tip the scales in favor of the good. That is why a person should consider themselves as if they were the one lone righteous person. The fate of the world might actually depend upon you."
>
> *--Zohar*

What do we desire? What do we want or perhaps need in order to live a meaningful life? Money? Love? Health? There are many things that we covet from race cars to vast fortunes. The choices are seemingly infinite. We are complex beings with so many needs and even more desires.

It may be a lot easier to gauge the opposite. We know what is bad for us. We may at least know what we do not want. We have learned what does not work from our experiences of failure. From those failures we have a reasonably developed sense of what is not good for us. For example, we know from experience what happens when we lie or steal. The punishment or fear of punishment is enough to make us wary before we do it. There is, of course, also the internal punishment for wrongs committed. An unremitting conscience can be a powerful deterrent.

Yet, the first and largest question remains, what makes us fulfilled people? What will satisfy us? Then what do we need to achieve that end?

In the last chapter, we focused on learning to unburden ourselves from the heavy load of prejudice, i.e. not relying on our knee-jerk reactions to people and situations but gazing at what our *mind* sees. Without that additional bulk weighing us down, life offers so much more possibility. Therefore, let us examine some of the lessons that life has taught us; lessons of incalculable worth. What follows are some questions that we already know the answer to and will help lift us to another level. Consider:

What makes the difference in our day whether we feel uplifted or afflicted? Try to recall those events which happened during the hours of waking that made us feel a sense of goodness. Naturally, every day will be different, but there are certain things that translate themselves into an overarching feeling of well-being. What are they? Someone allowing us to proceed before them in the check-out line? Giving another person the *right of way*? A good lunch? A letter from a friend? Writing an e-mail to a relative? A nice conversation? A good sale? A compliment from the boss? An act of charity? Being the recipient of someone's good-will or doling it out? Having nothing go wrong during the day?

If these questions are too difficult, let's again try from the opposite perspective. What fills us with a sense of dark brooding? When we have finished writing a nasty note to someone? Or when we feel a need to write it? An inconsiderate waiter? A flat tire? Someone who cuts in front of us in line? When we are quicker than they are to the empty parking space? Or when they beat us to the space? Someone making a cutting comment? A foul comment or action we made? Needing assistance and not getting it? Feeling as if nothing has gone right during the day?

A lot of these listed actions will have a powerful effect on us.

Some more than others. It is the 'more than others' that we ought to be concerned with here. There is a list of four categories in which we can place these feelings. The first two are "giver" and "receiver" of goodness. The second two are "victim" and "victimizer."

Initially, let us concentrate of the first pair; giving and receiving goodness. An easy example of the exchange of goodness is a compliment. On the one side is saying something nice to another person. The other side is having someone say something nice about or to, us. Both are good and nourish us. Yet of the two, which is preferable? Which gives a longer sense of satisfaction? Being the giver or receiver of the compliment? Which works better for us?

Being a clergyman is not an easy profession. It is probably one of the more difficult jobs to gain and maintain a sense of progress and satisfaction. In most professions there are specific criteria for success, like sales, processing data, dispensing medicine... One's performance can be easily gauged by what has been accomplished at the end of the day.

For the priest, minister or rabbi what is the litmus test for success? Early on in my career I assumed it had to be membership. The more members there were in my congregation the better I must be at its helm, I figured. I expended great energy to imagine and create programs and marketing schemes that would attract new blood. Yet, I quickly discovered that it was a deceptive barometer of success because quality of membership (activities, involvement, growth) may ultimately have little to do with numbers. What difference does it make to have full ranks but no internal growth? What was the point of having more people on the rolls if there was no upward movement towards greater involvement, participation, development and learning?

In some congregations, the membership may have already reached its zenith for its time. Simply, there may be no more prospective members at this moment. Trying to connect success with increased membership would be an exercise in self-flagellation.

Abandoning the idea that membership numbers was the baseline for my success or failure, I turned to the notion of an active congregation as a real indicator of my proficiency as a minister. I grew proficient in making programs for every interest group. That too, however, proved to be wrong-minded. A community that is kept busy is not necessarily a congregation of growth and learning and holiness. It is almost like an overbearing parent that believes their child must be constantly stimulated and active every hour of the waking day lest they lose their competitive edge. This kind of over-programming is self deception. Childhood is robbed of its many indefinable treasures in leaving little time for self reflection and individual discovery. The same applies to a congregation. The richness of quality educational and experiential programs is of far greater consequence than keeping busy.

I then realized that the more spiritual approach would be to accept that the minister's job may be as messenger to one person only. My job may be to link a single person to God, not necessarily as an outreach to the "un-churched." This too, had its negative side as it did not service the needs of the "congregation" as a whole. The Board of Directors would not be aware of such successes. Even if they did know about how individual lives were influenced, such life changes do not translate into documented, quantifiable growth.

These various indicators -- along with others -- of success are used by ministers and their congregations. How else to determine success than through numbers and a busy schedule? Many pastors have been summarily dismissed because they did not produce tangible figures on membership rolls or increase contributions. On the other hand, the community that accentuates personal observance and learning and places it above all else, may be a quality congregation, but that does not necessarily mean those spiritual changes are observable. If the bottom-line is the final arbiter of success, many ministers are doomed for disappointment. So ministers tend to be in a vise-grip of determining how to measure their success or failure. That is why one recent survey placed forty percent of its ministers as ready to leave their pulpits if they had enough financial security to do so.

So in the absence of any objective indicator of success, the minister lives off the comments of their parishioners. Their accolades or criticisms may build or demolish a rabbi's view of himself. One dear colleague confided, "I can live for a month off a good compliment." The opposite is **at least** as true. One withering comment can be devastating. That pastor's nourishment is dependent upon others. Is this us? Are we also needy? Do we require ongoing reinforcement to shore up our sense of being? Are we a needy receiver waiting to be restored to wholeness?

I call her "Ms. Perfect" although she does not know it. I often have found myself wishing I could clone "Ms. Perfect" and fill the pews and Board with people just like her.

Twice a week she goes to the hospital to visit the sick. She then calls me to let me know if someone needs extra attention. "Ms. Perfect" has been known to cook for patients who have been released to their home but have no one to take care of them. On the weekends, she leads Sabbath services at an old age home nearby. She sings for them, dances with them, holds frail hands, prays for them and teaches from the Bible. Whenever I need help in the congregation or community I know that I can rely on "Ms. Perfect" because the word "no" is not in her vocabulary. Countless times she has rescued people from the edge of oblivion.

I asked "Ms. Perfect" why she does it. She answered, "Because it feels good." End of conversation.

Knowing what makes us feel satisfaction allows us to achieve wholeness. So, returning to the initial question, which are you? Giver or receiver? Perhaps you might be both. Are both needed in equal measure? Or does one nourish the soul more than the other? Which of the two brings us a greater sense of well-being?

At least as important as the answer to these questions is identifying how to maintain a steady diet of what we need to ensure our psychic wellbeing. The minister described above is in constant need of stroking. Without that validation from others he may fall prey to depression. It seems infinitely easier to be a "Ms. Perfect" because then we can immerse ourselves in that behavior whenever we have a spare moment. Acts of goodness are dependent on no one, except ourselves. It is a position of empowerment, not of dependency.

It is easy to give a compliment. It is ridiculously simple to always keep change in our pocket in order to have it within reach when there is someone needy. It requires no talent or level of education to do a favor. These actions are a great deal easier than depending upon the compliments of others to feed our ego. That nourishment might not arrive for months! Or it might never come in the way that we imagine it to come. In that instance, we will be always disappointed. We have little control, if any, over being a receiver of goodness. The only control we really have is the goodness we dispense.

It is not only more noble to be a giver than a receiver, it is also a more wholesome way to live.

It is vital to be aware of the things we have control over and those where we are powerless. Why place faith and invest energy into relying on others to make us happy when that may never happen? In fact the opposite is just as likely to happen; they may excoriate us with a sharp tongue and harsh criticism. If we are dependent upon them for our self-esteem, we may become very disappointed and bitter. In fact, the most important consideration to think about may be what makes us happy. If a significant segment of our happiness requires us to "do good," why deny ourselves that privilege and gift?

The second dyad of being a victim or victimizer has the same set of questions attached to it. What causes the worst possible feeling in us? One simple example: what causes a more profound sense of loss? When someone criticizes us in a nasty, hurtful way? Or when we have been excessively critical to them? Which of the two has a longer pain-laden, residual feeling to it? Which is worse for you? Victim? Or victimizer?

Elie Wiesel, conscience to an entire generation, has asked the same question: Which category do you belong to, victim or victimizer? Whose side do you stand with? Everyone is faced with the decision of standing with or against the oppressor in their lifetime many times over. Either we aid the victimizer actively by persecuting and oppressing the innocent or stand by passively while they practice their evil. In either case, participating or watching the evil take place, Wiesel tells us, is the same. Evil only continues to exist, he explains, because it is tolerated. Turning a 'blind eye' to evil gives permission to the persecutors to continue. Tolerating evil is tantamount to performing the act. There is no such thing as remaining impartial in the face of evil. Remaining impartial means giving license to those who practice evil to continue their nefarious behavior.

Being on the side of the victim, Elie Wiesel explains, means that we do not stand idly by while blood is spilled or shame is thrust upon someone. Taking the side of the victim means that we protest. We yell. We scream and protest. We defy the evil, even when it is not in our best interest. Taking a position against evil can bring us suffering and pain. Everyone is called upon in their lives to take their place with one of the two sides: Victim or victimizer. Which are we? Which side have we taken?

I pose these questions with a great deal of trepidation and humility because answering them honestly will expose our deepest fears and weakest points of the psyche. People's compliments and approval may have become our sustenance, our bread. Some people are more needy than others and require more 'shoring up.' We are all affected by what others say to us and how we are treated. The biggest question is: to what degree do we let neediness control us? Likewise, disagreeing with evil and taking a stand against it can bring us suffering. The rationale for not becoming involved on the behalf of those who suffer is that we will also become the target for the victimizers.

Oskar Schindler is a name that should be universally recognized and studied by students of morality and history throughout the world. Schindler was a genuine hero. An inveterate womanizer, gambler and heavy drinker, there was nothing in his character or background to suggest that he could be a saint. Yet Schindler saved twelve hundred people from torture and murder at the hands of the Nazis.

When factories of death were being built, when houses of worship were burned to the ground, when the beards were ripped off the faces of old men in the street and Jews were taken from their homes and beaten relentlessly in the streets, ordinary citizens in Nazi occupied lands were called upon to make a choice. Most people were too frightened of choosing to be on the side of the victim. They too would be singled out for death.

One man, Schindler, made his decision choosing a different path. He risked his life, spent everything he had, even sold his wife's jewelry to save people whom he did not know. Why? Why would such a man act with such righteousness? Schindler himself answered, "There was no choice. If you saw a dog going to be crushed under a car, wouldn't you help him?"

Countless times every day we are called upon to make a choice about our identity. If we see day old bread being thrown out at the supermarket do we make an effort to get it into hungry hands? Do we know where to bring it? Would we make the effort to find out?

A question of attitude: Are beggars people who need help or are they to blame for their own condition and, therefore should be ignored? Do we let their car go in front of ours? Or do we cut them off? Do we complain that the clerk did not serve us well? Or do we compliment the one that does an excellent job? When a child is being hit do we turn away? Or do we stop and try to reason with the angry parent as a protector for the one who is being abused? The way we decide each of these scenarios - and countless more -- defines who we are. The decision not only determines which side we choose to stand with – victim or victimizer -- it also influences how we perceive ourselves. What we do creates self definition which may end up deciding whether we are satisfied with our life, or desperately unhappy.

We have all been victims and victimizers. Bertrand Russell once commented that, "Life is nothing but a competition to be the criminal rather than the victim." Russell voiced the most base of all human tendencies; to be the top dog (which is invariably standing on the back on the dogs beneath it). We know what it feels like to be a victim; it is not comfortable. I believe that Russell's observation though is overly pessimistic. We always have a choice and ultimately there is only a single problem to be solved: we need to be able to discern the difference between being a victim and victimizer. We can always choose to be a healer or destroyer. That is our primary task.

Within one week I had two separate appointments with a couple that had just been divorced. First, the woman came in with a haze of despair and a heaviness that was palpable. As soon as she entered, the room seemed to shift to dark clouds as she sat down on the couch in my study. Sarah told me of her cheating husband who lied to her, deceived and maligned her and ultimately stole all her dreams away. He was a criminal, she declared.

"He should be shot. He destroyed the home, the relationship, the kids, everything." Sarah cried, "There is nothing left inside of me. I am so angry some times that I want to scream! Other times, I feel so empty that I just do not want to get up in the morning. I don't want to eat or get dressed. This is hell. I am living in hell."

Later that same week, Vic made an appointment to see me. He came in and begged me to do something about Sarah. "I need your advice." Yes, he admitted, he had done her wrong. He had apologized to Sarah for it, gave her everything she wanted but "all she wants to do is skin me alive. What more can I do? Give me some advice," Vic implored. "I know that I have been unfaithful and have hurt Sarah. I will do whatever I can to do the right thing by her. But it can't go on forever…I can't take it!"

A few months later, Vic made another appointment. "You gotta do something. Sarah is out of her mind. She talks bad about me to the kids. She keeps slinging me back into court and even the judge is rolling his eyes every time we come back in. It is not just an embarrassment. It has gone well beyond that. There is nothing left. If she keeps this up I am going to have to start fighting back, hurting her."

Question: Who is the victim and who is victimizer? At first blush, having heard one side of the story, it seemed pretty clear to me. Yet, as time progressed the lines between Sarah and Vic began to blur and it became increasingly difficult to know who was the culprit: they both now had ample reason to be deeply wounded. They had done their utmost to galvanize their friends against the other, they used the kids as pawns trying to turn them against the other parent, and dragged the spouse through a string of endless court proceedings.

So much of Sarah and Vic's feud began to become opaque. It was difficult to know who was right and who was wrong. Often, there are shades of light and dark in everything. So, how do we deal with the *grays* of life, where there is not absolute right and wrong? Sometimes we just do not know who the victim is.

Let's determine what we **do** know.

1. We know that good and evil happens only in relationships between people and people or people and things. Atrocities and saintly acts do not happen in nature. Only humans are capable of creating good and evil. People alone are moral.

2. Earlier we learned that heaven and earth are mirror images of one another. What happens in one place will have its corollary in the other.

3. Next we learned a second point is that everything in a single dimension, that is, our universe, is also connected. No event is self-contained; every action has a ripple effect that radiates outward and has far-reaching effects. We are all much more important that we know. We, therefore, have a role in every passive or active event. Even if we do nothing, that inaction also impacts the outside world. We are interconnected with everything. Ergo, we have some control over the outcome of every situation.

In every moment of life there are seeds ready to germinate and emerge. These are seeds of blessing or curse, goodness or evil. Vic and Sarah were to blame in different ways. It may be difficult to isolate one of them as utterly evil and the other as wholly good. However, we can separate out acts and identify them as kind or hurtful. The task of their true friends is to be aware enough to point out where righteous indignation transforms into vindictiveness and evil. Vic and Sarah embodied both principles of goodness and evil. Our job is to separate them out. Taking a stand where morality is concerned is not always comfortable (it is rarely simple or easy) yet there is a backwash which brings great light to the universe and, in this instance, our soul.

We began this chapter with a metaphor of a scale or balance. On one side of the scale is goodness while the other side holds evil. They may be perfectly balanced. A moment may come when it is in our hands to make the ultimate difference in the way the scales tip. Are we prepared for that moment? Have we successfully considered who we are and what our place is in the world as doer/receiver of goodness and victim/victimizer?

Remember that Kabbalah holds that every person has a spark of infinite radiance in them. As the Deuteronomy quote at the beginning of the chapter indicates, our reaction to the universe, acting in harmony with God, grants total and true life. How then do we know when we are listening to God and acting in accord with the Ultimate Will? Or merely listening to the voice which tells us to act out of self-interest? The answer can be found in the clear and candid responses to the questions below. In answering them we learn who we are and then, if we act upon this knowledge, we begin to tread the path of making the difference in tipping the celestial scale.

1. What nourishes our sense of self worth? Being in a position of giving? Being able to receive? Which of these two aspects best defines our character? Which gives us a more fulfilled sense of being alive, giving or receiving? Once we have defined who we are through a severe introspective look at our self, it then follows we must literally ask ourselves, "Is this what I want?" "Is this who I want to be?" "Do I like what I have learned about myself?"

2. In acting out our impulses, our responses to life, are we active participants or passive bystanders? What do we bring to the daily table of life? Is the world better today because we trafficked through it? Is it the same? Is it worse? Ask: "If I were to die today what ripples would I leave behind as a legacy?"

Realizing who we are and what we need to feel whole is the path of understanding our core self. It is also the way of fulfillment and joy. Only when we understand who we are can we gain control over our lives. Just as there are necessary vitamins and minerals that we need to stay healthy, so too, there is a specific kind of nourishment that the *neshama*, soul, hungers for. It is the point of connection where we may be touched by God and feel the kiss of the Divine.

There is a place and time for all things: Giving and receiving are choices that we make and have. It is soulfully important to know who we are and what is our place in the universe. Equally important is to recognize the difference between a victim and victimizer and the apparent shades that exist in the space of inaction. We need to know who we are before we act in consonance with God and soul.

א א א א א

A large part of this book has been oriented around reading old familiar texts with fresh new insight. That is the way of the mystic. For the Kabbalist nothing is as it appears. Kabbalah supposes that the Bible (like everything else) is far more than it appears. At first glance the Bible is a series of stories that outline the theology and history of religious life in the world. A more detailed examination of the Bible yields other fruits. In other words, the Bible begs to be read and understood more deeply.

For example. The Tower of Babel seems to indicate the origin of disparate cultures and languages. The face reading of the Text:

Babel tells the story of a massive undertaking by humanity to raise a tower that would reach the portals of heaven. The people devised a plan to storm the realm of God and wrest control of the cosmos. God, divining the evil portent of the citizens of Babel, determined that humanity needed to be scattered and varied to prevent such misdirected and wrongful occurrences in the future. The penalty for Babel is the subsequent *babble* of languages that prevent further and future building.

While this is a reasonable surface reading of the Bible, it is only an apparent exterior reading. To read the Babel narrative on a deeper level would be to see it as an attempt to speak to the heart of humanity, urging it to work together for good purposes, not evil. This assessment of the Tower story is also true but only penetrates the first skein of understanding of a complex reading of the Bible. Another yet deeper layer of the mystic reading is to try to understand the metaphoric meaning of the Text. Kabbalah's home is here.

A kabbalistic reading of the Babel narrative has the second sentence of the tale in Genesis as highly revealing of the inner intent of the text... and almost invisible. It states, "And they journeyed from the east..." Those same words in the original Hebrew could just as easily be translated as, "And they journeyed from their beginnings...". In this second rendition, the people of Babel are deliberately walking away from their roots. In other words, the people were seeking idols to replace God.

Pursuing this idea further, the mystical text remembers that humanity was created in the image of God. What does this mean? That we are supposed to work to create wholeness on earth just as the Holy One endeavors to make whole the expanse beyond. In building the Tower, humanity was rejecting its holy task of perfecting the world. It was abdicating the true intent of the Master for His creation. The real sin of Babel was that humanity was walking away from its responsibility to be humane. The world depends upon our actions. We can doom the world by the choices we make. Alternatively, we can redeem it. That is our gift. And our challenge.

Let's review: Getting up in the morning is usually accompanied by a long list of things to do. We may have to go shopping, fix a leaky faucet, pay the mortgage, go to work…each of us wakes with a focus, a direction, a purpose at the beginning of the day. The list may be a physical one; it may be just the things we realize throughout the day that are critical; or the list may be contrived. Shouldn't it also be part of our daily regime to focus on think about these tasks and prioritize them?

If giving to others reinforces our sense of balance and wellbeing, our day ought to incorporate an attitude, and perhaps even planned events, where we do acts of helping people. That may be a more important function, in fact, than the sales meetings or fixing the leaky faucet, as it may have a dramatic emotional impact on our day, our personal interactions and on the way we view ourselves and feel at the end of the day. It may change our outlook and inner sense of psychic and moral health.

What we do impacts the outer universe. How we do it… impacts our inner universe.

With the internal understanding that our lives really do matter because of the potential power that we wield, comes the idea that we are called to make changes. Our mandate is to fix the broken and leaky pipes of the world, to intervene with the usual machinations of the time and people and please the Master. Of course, this must be predicated on acknowledging and developing a relationship with God. Once we have accepted that we require and thrive on relationships, the next natural step is to move those lateral significant relationships to a vertical plane.

Just the act of getting up in the morning is not enough; it is how we mete out our day's tasks as well as what we do with our gifts that makes all the difference. There is a place for everything. The focal point is you.

Chapter 3

Scheduling

The ears of the Holy One. Everything emanates from the sound that comes to the ears; it [the sound] enters the whole body and everything trembles from it. Much is derived from that ear. Blessed is the person who guards what they say. That is why it is written in Psalms, "Keep your tongue from evil, and your lips from speaking guile" (34:14).

--Zohar

Leviticus 19:15 states, "Do not place a stumbling block before the blind. The Zohar interprets, "Nothing uttered by a human being will not be heard. Further, that sound will ascend on High. As that uttered sound continues its upward journey it is joined by Angels of Destruction. Finally, the nuanced sound will come to place of the Great Chasm, the place where the holy vessels can be found. They are then roused against the One ...."

Who doesn't want to slow down? Better yet, who doesn't *need* to slow down? Every invention that comes along to simply our lives, make us more productive, serves the opposite end.

Jonathan M. Case

Have events outpaced your ability to keep up with them? Is the vehicle you are traveling in is going much too fast? Does the sheer velocity of this free-fall maintain itself regardless of what you do? The momentum that we worked so hard to achieve propels us forward, whether we want to move or not. All efforts go into holding onto the steering wheel in a desperate attempt to keep the car from careening out of control. It becomes harder, almost impossible, to brake.

That is why vacations have become so urgent for our culture. Holidays, cruises, bike trips, hikes and rafting adventures remove us from the relentless stimuli that urge us on at a soul-consuming, unforgiving pace. Finally, our fingers can unclench their fierce grip on the steering wheel! Yet, I wonder: Has it ever happened that even your vacations seem to mimic life at home? Are holidays also over-scheduled? Too many things to do? Too many places to see? "Grab the camera." "Grab the kids. The tour leaves in five minutes! Hurry!" "We need to get up early tomorrow if we want to see the rain forest.".... Do you come back from vacation tired and needing a break?

Scheduling issues are most often seen as a business concern. The vehicle races along at a breakneck speed. A red light. The client is waiting for his appointment. The secretary calls in sick. The boss delays getting materials to us on time which causes us stress. More problems mean more energy needs to go into more ingenious solutions. Is there 'dead weight' not doing their share in the organization? An angry client calls and excoriates the nearest person on a headset. The computer is down and suddenly everyone in the office is immobilized. Frozen faces give way to panic....

Most of the issues that come to us are not critical. How many times could other responsible people answer those issues? Petty problems require petty, or simple, solutions. Still, petty solutions to petty problems can sap energy and erode our strength, if there are enough of them. They can become an encumbrance, a burdensome weight. Small problems are like gnats: After a while, they annoy the flesh so much that all we want to do is run away screaming.

The answer to over-scheduled work problems sounds easy: Less appointments and more time in between engagements will yield enough time to rest and consider decisions carefully. Then can we integrate the information we have absorbed and take appropriate action. A good organized person can sort out the conundrum of time rather quickly. Or, if we have enough determination and focus, we can put our energy and creative talents toward smoothing out the staccato blur of life. The same is true for life at home, life on vacation and perhaps even the life that happens in our dreams. We already possess the skills to slow the pace of life. Reality does not often jibe with the simple solution, though. For many people considering change is far easier than implementing it. If the easy answer has not worked for you; if you bounce right back to where you were before after a brief period of 'down-time;' you need something else. The "something else" is the holy moment.

How would our day be different if we could rid our cluttered day of those annoying hindrances? The ones which eat up so much of our valuable time and, more importantly, our energy? The ones where we find ourselves repeating what we have said for the fifth time (and growing less patient with each rendition)?

Let me share a sacred story about the sacred moment. I have busy days, some more than others. There are those days when appointments are back to back with no breaks or relief. One Monday stands out in my memory as particularly forgettable. My secretary had scheduled meetings all morning and afternoon long with no breathing space. Coffee in hand, I looked over my schedule I sighed. It was going to be one of *those* days. I braced myself for the onslaught and drank another cup of coffee for encouragement.

The day started with a meeting for the month's upcoming events. The second appointment of my still-early morning was with Linda. She came in with her three young children. The kids were alternately crying, picking up items off my desk, throwing them on the floor and banging on the fish tank. I cringed. I tried to ignore the children and focus on Linda who had settled in one of the deep creases of the couch and stared down at her lap.

"Frank didn't come home last night," she began in a monotone. It almost sounding like Linda was reading a dull article from the newspaper. "His car was not in the driveway. No bowls or dishes in the sink. So, I looked in the closet. His clothes were missing."

Words began to come out punctuated by catches in her voice. Tears leaked unnoticed, unchecked, from her eyes. The kids had become invisible and were suddenly quiet.

"I don't know what to do. He left me with nothing. I should

have seen it coming because of the way he was behaving lately. His mood had changed. He wasn't really interested in anything the kids or I did….he was just there….it is as if he had already left us….

"You know, I haven't worked in six years. I don't know what I am going to do. The kids need me constantly. They ask me where daddy is and I don't know what to tell them. I know how to handle them. I always have. But now there are piles of bills to pay. The mortgage is due next week. Help me. What should I do?"

I mostly listened and let Linda talk. She continued for a long time. I held her hands and tried to find some meaningful words to encourage her. All the while she was speaking, my mind was racing trying to think of things to do, a key person to call on her behalf, something that would give Linda hope. Even more, I was attempting to come up with a solution to even one of Linda's overwhelming problems. With my mind turning over every conceivable option, I asked Linda about what led up to this, where her support system would come from in the future, a hodgepodge of questions that might give me an insight or flash realization of some contribution I could make to alleviate her misery.

"Isn't there anyone you can depend on for some help?" I asked.

Linda responded that she had her mother but she was very old. Linda's father was deceased. She had a few close friends but no one that she could really trust. There was no one to depend on. She cried a lot. We explored different possibilities. I wrote down some numbers for her to call for assistance. At the end of our session, we hugged.

"You are going to be alright," I told her. "Your children are much stronger than you think and they have a rock for a mother who will not abandon them. By you just surviving, you are giving them the most powerful, unspoken message of their life. Do not be surprised that this experience will give them great strength in years to come. For now, just don't give up."

I encouraged Linda to find a reliable sitter, get a job and recommended a competent lawyer. It was a very painful hour for me. When the door closed behind her, I collapsed into my chair. I was drained and felt helpless. As much as Linda told me how much better she was having come in, I felt miserable that I could not help her more. I wished that I could have given her some physical assurance that everything would be alright....

This was one of those occasions when I wish I had a break in the schedule to decompress, just run out the door. Spend some time with my friends. There was no time, though. This was one of those days.

My next appointment announced by the secretary was with Dave. I knew him well. Dave was a joker and bon vivant. He was the sort of fellow that you would like to invite to your party as he kept a lively conversation flowing and people laughing. I really wished he had cancelled the appointment or would have just disappeared. I was not in the mood for his inevitable buoyancy. Neither, as it turned out, was possible.

When Dave came in, he bounced in with a sly look on his face. Dave was very happy, even for Dave. He began, "I sit on a philanthropic board with some friends and colleagues. Yearly, we give two thousand dollars to a worthy cause in the community. I brought up your Discretionary Fund to the board because I know that you do lots of good things with the money. So, I'd like to present you with this check to make good use of." He extended his hand with the check.

That was a holy moment in the midst of a maelstrom.

An over-scheduled day that I was dreading found a kernel of redemption in it. That moment was a holy moment because God went out of His celestial way to use me as an instrument of intervention in the lives of Linda and Dave. My eyes widened as I realized I could call Linda on her cell phone and tell her, before she even got home, the good news. The moment was not just the bridging of two people who had needs that uncannily connected them. That alone was beyond poignant and serendipitous. It would have been enough, I realized, had nothing of this sort happened. It was a moment for me to find where and who I was. I smiled. The good humor lasted me the long day and well beyond.

Truer yet is that day - and every other day --is pock-marked with holy moments but my face had been forced to see just this one. Miracles are surely in the eye of the beholder. The only question is, does anyone see them?

"Kabbalah" means "receiving." No one can receive something unless they open their hearts, open their minds and sometimes open their hands. Receiving is reciprocal; there must be both a Giver and someone to receive the gift.

| Idea: we cannot take something if our hands are clenched. |

The way of Kabbalah is the way of openness so that we are always in a state of preparedness to receive. Openness to the One and to the myriad of miracles that abound in every day. One of the most important segments of Kabbalah is becoming aware so that realize when a gift is being presented. A primary tenet of Kabbalah is that the Divine energy always flows. The Gift is ever-present. There is only one outstanding question: Is there anyone claiming it?

Two hundred years ago, American sage and wit, Benjamin Franklin, understood the idea of needing to be aware of each moment when he stated, "For the want of a nail, the shoe was lost; for the want of a shoe the horse was lost; and for the want of a horse the rider was lost, being overtaken and slain by the enemy, all for the want of a horseshoe nail."

There is nothing insignificant about life. No matter is too small to be part of the great circle that encompasses all. Even a nail can be of ultimate consequence. In the Book of the Zohar there is a teaching that reads: "Israel should make themselves partners with God; walking and waking. It is written: "When you walk, it will lead you; when you lie down, it will keep you; and when you awake, it will talk with you" (Proverbs 6:22). The student hearing these profound words rose, bowed low and said: Happy is the portion of he who is worthy of hearing these words, which are all the Name of the Lord."

The meaning of the teaching? *Do not sleep at the wheel.*

Simply to be awake is one of the prime operating factors of mysticism. The Zohar is not saying to us that we cannot physically sleep. It is telling us that when we are awake we must be fully engaged in the world. When we are awake we must be awake. Only in a state of watchfulness can we be aware enough of each act to gauge the meaning of what is being spoken; of each action taken. So much of being fully alive is bound up with just the obvious and simple task of remaining awake.

There is no multi-tasking in a state of awareness. There is no multi anything. There is only the holy moment. It is not possible to be overwhelmed by life when we are totally, utterly present and awake. All extraneous, competing thoughts of what we need to do in the next ten minutes, checks that need to be written, dishes that require cleaning do not interfere in a moment of utter awareness. They do not exist.

Remember the punch line of the joke that has gone bad? Nobody laughs so the joke-teller says, "You had to be there." Let's revise that slightly for our purpose: **You need to be here**. There is nowhere else to be other than in this moment. There is only one voice in the present-tense. There are no conflicts.

Think of a state of half-awareness, when our attention is divided. Is it possible to hear the underlying message if we are only listening to the words? Imagine the difficulty of listening to a conversation when the facial expressions are obscured. Half-listening without a full awareness of the body language, the eye movements and the nuanced inflections is akin to being partially blind. We are prone to miss the real message. In a state of being awake, we can fully hear what is being said. Hearing only the spoken word, watching only the facial expressions, not listening with the heart is to be in some measure asleep. We might as well not be there at all because the message they bring may be totally distorted by our partial understanding.

I enjoy the highway announcements telling drivers to be aware if they feel sleepy. Some rest stops even host kind-hearted folks serving coffee to weary travelers. Why not? Most personal-sized vehicles weigh in at about 3,000 pounds. SUV's and larger cars will weigh much more. That means that every person is driving a potential bomb, a weapon that can ruin scores of lives on the road. Being awake on the road sounds like a good idea to me. It sounds even better if it works for the rest of our waking hours.

The human mouth is every bit as dangerous as an out-of-control piece of steel weighing one ton. Isn't that what the first quote at the beginning of this chapter really means about being attentive to all sounds as everything is heard elsewhere? To be wholly, fully engaged in the universe is to live a vital, meaningful existence. To be partially engaged is to give an illusion of being wakeful while we are sleeping life away. I believe that more lives are ruined because the person we are trying to talk to is asleep than bad drivers who cause ruinous physical injury on the roads. Perhaps we ought to consider starting a new campaign in very office and coffee klatch throughout the country:

➢ Stay awake: The messiah is right behind you. Or…

> Drink coffee: You never know when someone might say the phrase that will alter your life. Forever. Or…
> Pay attention: Someone in this room knows how to solve your vexing work problem. But only *one* of them knows this secret. Listen. Or…
> Quick: This is the last time you will ever see this person in this moment ever. Or…
> Someone is about to die. Say what needs to be said now!

The holy Zohar renders a fantastic and remarkable tale:

The sage Elazar was walking in the fields when a dove flew directly toward him and settled on his arm. The dove cooed into the famed teacher's ear that his father-in-law, Yossi, was mortally ill. Rabbi Elazar then told the dove to reassure his father-in-law that he would be well and that Elazar and his colleagues would come to his home to celebrate his recovery.

The dove then flew off to his destination and later returned to the teacher, Elazar. This time, nestling on his shoulder, the bird whispered, "The Angel of Death would not be assuaged. Since you had overruled his decree, the Angel of Death has taken another victim in his stead. Your father-in-law lives but another Yossi, from the village of Pekiyin, has been taken."

Hearing the message, Elazar was distraught. He set out to the town of to Pekiyin to comfort this Yossi's family. Feeling responsible, he wanted to provide solace to the grieving and take part in the burial of the man and comfort his survivors.

When Elazar and the entourage finally arrived in Pekiyin they were told that the recently deceased Yossi was survived by two children, a young son and daughter. "No wife?" the sage wondered. "No mother to care for the two children?" This family had known deep pain. The man's wife died a short time before. Now there were two young orphans and no one to watch over them.

Elazar approached the bier containing the body. The son refused to budge from his deceased father's side. He lay on the bed with him and cried and cried until his chest heaved from the dry pain of exhaustion. The boy had laid his head close to his father and his ragged breath caught. He looked upward and rasped, "Master of the Universe, You wrote in your holy Bible:

192

'If you find a bird's nest, in a tree or on the ground, with fledglings or eggs, and the mother is sitting over the fledglings or on the eggs, you may not take the mother together with her young. Let the mother go and take only the young.'

He wept, "Master of the Universe! According to your holy Word, the mother must live. *We* are not allowed to take the mother bird and leave the children alone, orphaned. That is what You said! You, God, must also fulfill the words of Your holy Bible, the words You spoke. My sister and I are like the two little birds. My mother is dead and only our father was able to take her place to care for us. According to You, dearest God, You may take either me or my sister, but You may not take away my father!"

The venerable teachers heard the boy's plaintive cry. Elazar and his colleagues wept with him.

In the moments after the child uttered those words the house became very still. It was as if a giant glass bell had been placed over the house. No sound was heard. The room was silent as a pillar of white fire descended from the heavens and began to hover over the bed of the dead father. Everyone was seized with an unnamable terror.

Elazar, quiet awe in his voice, said, "A great miracle is about to occur."

Out of that flaming column of light came a heavenly voice: "You are a blessed father, Yossi, to merit such a son whose bitter pain has pierced the Gates of Heaven, ascending directly to God's Throne of Glory. A new verdict has been passed. Yossi will live twenty-two more years. He will have the privilege of raising and teaching this wise child."

As suddenly as it had come, the pillar disappeared. Yossi's eyes opened.

Elazar exclaimed, "We to have witnessed with our own eyes the miracle of the dead returning to life! Tell me, Yossi, what did you see?"

Yossi replied, "I cannot reveal everything I have seen. It is beyond me. I can only share with you this: When my son was pleading, weeping and protesting to God from the depths of his being, and mentioned His commandment of sending the mother bird away, three hundred thousand heavenly chairs shook. Three hundred thousand righteous souls stood up in that other world, begging God to return me to the land of the living!"

This story is fantastic. It dwells beyond the reach of belief. Yet, what is the purpose of the story? What does it mean? Why does this ancient mystic book tell us this tale? Is it good story-telling? Is it merely a quaint tale about love and God's power? Or is there something more?

There is a strong underlying message to the story: God wants to be engaged. Perhaps the worst sin for the *homo religiousus,* the truly religious person, is to not be angry with God, argue, or even curse God, but ignore Him. God wants His children to take an interest and open their mouths and their ears with an openness to connect with the One. The tale underscores the fierce human need to be awake and connected while telling us that if we desire a connection to God we must first be alert. Life becomes so much more vibrant when we are aware of ourselves and the world around us. Is this true?

A colleague of mine told the following tale many years ago: A motorist was barreling down the interstate when he saw blue lights flashing in his rear-view mirror. Pulling over to the side of the road, the driver decided to play ignorant.

"What's the matter, officer? Why are you stopping me?"

The policeman asked him if he saw the deer about one hundred feet back.

"No, officer I did not. What does that have to do with pulling me over?" he replied.

"What about the field of wildflowers in the median strip just before that?" he queried. "No, I didn't."

"That," said the officer, "is why I am stopping you."

Let's review: 'Take life and time seriously' is the first step to scheduling the day. Earlier, we learned about the need for thoughtful contemplation (see chapter two of the second section) in order to gain a more balanced view of life. Practiced daily, thoughtful contemplation forces us to move with greater care and appreciation: We see the world in a purer, more refined light. The world actually appears to be brighter.

We can hire or assign someone to intervene in our day's schedule (a secretary, planner) but it may ultimately make no impact on our *gestalt,* our way of traversing through time, until we have re-learned the fine art of being fully alive. Stop. Look.

Racing through the day may be the signal to our soul that we are unhappy. We want to get through our appointments quickly because they are tiresome tasks that needed to be meted out so that we have time to get to the "good stuff." Running at such a pace mans there will be no 'good stuff'. The 'good stuff' is now. Incessantly rushing is both unhealthy living as well as a gross misuse of the gift of time. Perhaps it is best to be where we are settled. Wherever we sit is where we ought to be.

There are many reasons why prayer occupies such a conspicuous role in all religions. One example is saying a prayer before we eat. Those kinds of prayers are integral because they force us to appreciate the food before we consume it. Prayer makes us cognizant of the gift of life. Prayer tells us to look at the physical world and find awe in the ordinary. In other words, prayer delivers a hidden message to the pray-er that states, "Slow down." "Listen to another human being with all your senses." "Consider the depth of beauty that inheres in all things."

Someone adept at prayer also has learned two key fundamental elements of being alive: One is to voice what is in their soul and the other is a refined art of listening in the sacred moment.

The ultimate solution to discovering the secret of a meaningful day or life is to be awake. Problems with scheduling the hours of our day is a **symptom** of how well or poorly we navigate through the awareness of life. Nothing in this universe is meaningless. Nothing is random. The ear that hears is the ear that is also attentive to the gnat, the unfolding leaf, Linda's cry to be healed and the pointed moment that waits us.

Chapter 4

Zeal

> Those who are truly deserving in this world are the ones who stand in awe of their Master. Their eyes will be enabled to witness three moments of absolute delight; the fusion or uniting of *Nefesh, Ruach* and *Neshama* in the World-to-Yet-to-Arrive.... Rabbi Simon said: You are each blessed, my children, as am I, that my eyes have seen that many heavenly places have been prepared for us in the World-to-Yet-to-Arrive.
>
> *--Zohar*

Some people laugh too loudly. You have heard them in the movie theatre, in the office and in the elevator. What about those who dance in the aisles of the local supermarket? And the weirdoes who seem to sparkle and glow as they smile passing through the canned food section of the supermarket? Were you ever fortunate enough to have run into one of those types?

What about those who seem to be perpetually having a good time? People think, "I wonder what they're taking?!" We *know* that people cannot be *that* happy; therefore something must be wrong with them. Maybe it's drugs or a 'screw loose.' Then there are those who have no clue about privacy; they just chatter loudly away in any venue as if the whole earth is eager to listen to their story.

All of these kinds of people share one common trait: They do not depend on other people's opinions of them to tell them how to behave. Whether they are nuts or obtuse or just totally comfortable with themselves, they remain unconcerned with what others think of them. They are living a life fully engaged in the moment.

Most people take their clues on behavior from what society deems the norm, squashing their inclinations. In other words, before leaping we look around to see who is watching. Then, and only then, do we decided to leap or stay put. A few examples:

The funeral of the young woman was held in a local chapel. She lived far too few years and, at the end of her life, suffered greatly from cancer. As the officiant, I came dressed in my usual stock black suit and somber tie. The service began with some ancient prayers that start to focus the mind of the mourners on the meaning of their loss and remembrance. All the while, I could hear the mother sniffling and emitting a few pain-riddled sighs. When I looked up I could not help but notice the nervous relatives seated around the mother alternatively putting their hands on her shoulders, handing her tissues, some rolling eyes, saying "shush, shush" and the like.

When the eulogy began and I mentioned the dead woman's name, this mother emitted a howl. The chapel was silent in the aftermath of her wail of pain. She went on crying so loudly that everyone, including me, stopped for a moment. After her wailing subsided a bit, I continued on with my words. The mother, crying and moaning over her loss, went on with her throaty inarticulate sobs, albeit slightly softer than before.

"Someone give her something!" I heard a person near the front mutter. More shushes. More words. More crying. The tension in the first few rows began to rise and I felt them like a slowly building wave. I looked up from the podium. They were literally sitting on the edges of their chairs casting not-so-covert glances over at the bereft mother.

When the old woman began to get up, however, is when the family decided to intervene. Several family members got up and caught her arms as she was panting her way toward the coffin of her daughter.

"It is all right," I said breaking stride from the eulogy. "She is voicing the pain that we all feel. It is real. It is genuine. Come to the bier with her," I directed the relatives in the front row. I walked down from the podium to meet and gather with the family members. "Stand with her. Wrap your arms around each other. She needs you now. We all need one another. What has happened is beyond painful. It is tragic. I believe even the Holy One cries now. Comfort her. Be with her and one another. Her tears are more real, more genuine than anything anyone could ever hope to say."

Question: Why should we hold back our grief? Because it might "embarrass" someone? Because we will look like we have lost control? Who cares? Death is the final exit from this world. There will be no more meetings. No more midnight rendezvous' at the refrigerator. No more cards, letters or calls. No more hugs, screams, caresses... The mother's reaction was right. In fact, her reaction was the most genuine and real of the many bewildered hundreds who gathered at that funeral. Why then was everyone else so focused on decorum when the heavens ought to have poured out its rage?

Some people call it love. Others call it rapture. Still others refer to it as ecstasy, head-over-heels. No matter the descriptive term, people who feel such raw, intense emotion are liable to express it without thought of how others will perceive it. There is a time when people "fall" in love and lose their perspective. They act out of their well of emotions and not like their usual self. Why should it be held back? For fear that someone will think us odd? Strange? That is not how love behaves. Love is open, honestly spoken and delivered. The most beautiful expressions of love are the impetuous ones.

I ask couples who have been married a long while, how and where they decided to become engaged. "How did you propose?" I will typically ask a couple who are celebrating their thirty-fifth or fiftieth anniversary how it all began. One pair answered that they chose the top of a mountain in Vermont (with skis on) to formalize their commitment. Another had a famous announcer at a baseball stadium "pop" the question. Yet another deftly hid a ring at the bottom of her dessert. Thank God she was looking at the dish when she raised the spoon to her mouth. My favorite was the skywriter...

Just as love is not ashamed to publicly proclaim its amorousness, so it was with the prophets of long ago. Whether we read from Ezekiel, who was so overcome with the vision of God that he was stupefied by what he saw, or by the tireless exhortations of Elijah who goaded idolaters and their cronies with soapbox speeches and tirades; the common bond between these prophetic men and women is that their ideas and communications were not informed by conventional propriety. They felt strongly, zealously about morality and God and they voiced the words of their conscience. Like the couples in love, they too were in a state of ecstatic emotion. There was no disconnect between what they felt to be true and how they acted upon what they believed.

Why should our lives be so detached as to segment our feelings into different spheres? Can't joy and zeal be hallmarks of a unified life? Why do have to "tone things down?" For the individuated person there is no such compartmentalization. The love they feel for life is mimicked by the love they feel in and through their life.

As discussed earlier in the book, love can be horizontal or vertical. At the horizontal axis, the greatest moments shared between lovers are the spontaneous, open ones. They are moments when foolishness wins over convention. Once upon a time we acted on these impulses. That is why they call it "head over heels" or "falling in love." Remember when we blurted out, "I am mad about you" or "I am desperately in love?" Each of these terms denotes acting on impulse, unconcerned with how our words or deeds are perceived by others. All that mattered was that the object of our affection heard us, understood the depth of our feeling. Those moments are remembered forever. Did that ecstatic state leave us? Is it gone? Why do we not behave that way any more? Loss of hormones? Or is it still there somewhere? Could it be buried deeply but so fearful of rejection and ridicule that we quell any potential outburst?

It works much the same way on the vertical axis. The emotions that we feel about goodness and God can be every bit as compelling as what we experience when we fall in love with another person. Point to remember: Do not obscure or minimize the difference between zealousness and evil. Just as there are people who attach themselves to others to an extent where the other person is hurt (think of the lover's quarrel that ends up with a gun shot) there are religious folks who act with equal impunity and cause great harm (think of suicide bombers). That is an evil act by any standard. The fact that there are people who commit such atrocities does not dismiss the reality of love nor should it diminish the intensity of our wonderful demonstrations of love.

In both directions, horizontally and vertically, we can experience and act upon our deepest emotions. Why shouldn't people do the watoosie next to the tuna fish cans in the supermarket? If we saw old people dancing in the isles, we would smile and enjoy their foot-work. It seems to me a tragic waste of the best years of our life when we are brimming with energy, vitality and youth that we wait until our advanced years to release our inner joy. Why must we wait until we grow old to act in accord with our heart?

I have told and studied stories for many years. There are stories which teach morals; some which leave exposed an emotional ques-tion which the listener is left to confront; others which depict a part of the psyche in anthropomorphic terms and some which just plain entertain. Of all the tales I have told and heard in my life one stands out above the rest:

The saint and sage Baal Shem Tov asked a favor of the One. "God, Master of All, can you show me my partner in the next world? Who will I be privileged to sit next to at the Divine Table for eter-nity? Lord, may I know who this man is?"

The Holy One then whispered the partner's name into the Baal Shem's ear. Now curious, the Baal Shem packed a few items into a bag and set out. On the journey to find this righteous individual, the Baal Shem Tov anticipated what a great person this must be; learned, kind, generous and understanding. He even imagined what such a fine individual might look like; tall – exuding strength - but ex-tremely gentle; strong to resist the forces of evil yet thoughtful enough to not hurt anyone.

After a very long trek of many days, the Master, Baal Shem, ar-rived at the place where he would find the one named by the Holy One. He found himself in a large meadow where two long hills met at the center. At the vortex of these hills moved a small stream two meters wide. Opposite, at the top of one of the hills stood a mo-tionless shepherd. He steadied himself and, as the Baal Shem Tov watched, the shepherd ran swiftly down the side of the hill towards the ravine. Just as his feet touched the side of the stream, the shep-herd hurled himself into the air. As he was midway across the water he screamed, "This is for You God!"

"This is the man I am destined to spend eternity with? An unedu-cated and simple farmer who spends his days shouting and running down in a ravine?" thought the Baal Shem.

The Baal Shem Tov continued to gaze as the shepherd gathered his strength and walked up the other side and once more ran down the hill yelling out the words, "This is for You God!" as he leaped across. The Baal Shem debated with himself as he viewed the simple, uneducated man repeating the same action time and again. Maybe I came to the wrong place? Perhaps I heard the name incorrectly.

After his initial shock and disbelief that this was the man with whom he would share eternity's table, the Baal Shem Tov finally began to smile. Understanding came to him. It would be a great privilege to be with someone so full of love for God.

That is all. That is the end of story. Unlike all the other stories I have heard and told, this one appeals only to a very select group of people who can understand and envy the companion of the Baal Shem for his utter love and devotion to God. To be whole and demonstrative in one's desire may be the ultimate dream and fulfillment of every spiritual person. To cast off all ideas about what is appropriate behavior to gain favor in other people's eyes is the final step of maturity and liberation.

Nefesh, Ruach and *Neshama* were discussed at length in the first section of this book. Maturity gains a firm hold of us when we come to realize what we need to become a whole person and then work to translate that idea into a living reality. Sublimating or dampening the highest emotions we possess leads to a fragmented or brokenness of self. That is why the simple shepherd is so enviable: He is at ease with his feelings of love and yearning. They are the expressions of his soul. He is the man whom we have seen pray at a holy site whose body convulses with feeling. We have seen him shout paeans of adoration like a madman only to make us smile with envy before we turn away out of self-embarrassment and absorption. We have watched her as she unabashedly hugs and kisses her dearest friend in the middle of the mall.

Despite what we might think about religious traditions and behavior, we do not jettison our esthetic sense of the world. If God had meant for us to be only souls, He could have stopped before they were folded into our bodies. The *nefesh*, or husk of our being, is integral to our existence and must also be cared for and nourished. And not merely for its own sake. Each segment of our self is indispensable to the rest.

Here is one example. Immerse yourself in a Sabbath. Once it was the backbone of our society. Stores closed for the holy day. In America, states established "blue laws" to guard trespassing against Sunday. Observant Jews likewise shuttered their businesses on their Sabbath. Such acts firmly established in their minds that something was more important than productivity: Life.

Having become an obstacle to the pursuit of "more," we did away with the Sabbath and the restrictive "blue laws." There was something profound and irreplaceable to the wisdom and practices of those who came before us. Take one day a week to feed the *nefesh* and during that time devote energy towards learning, praying and looking. While taking this one day out of our week will not necessarily make us more efficient at business (there are no guarantees here) and it goes against what society encourages (the national work ethic is more, not less); our *nefesh* and *neshama* needs more than what it receives in this universe to be completely human.

There is more to you than the one that gazes back at you from the mirror! A great part of the Sabbath is allowing the *nefesh* and its higher components enough opportunity to gain a glimpse of that eternal nature that abides within. While we learned earlier about the levels of soul, now we turn towards accessing and integrating what we have learned. What good is it to know we need to be happy? The question for modernity is: Is there a value to knowledge that has no physical expression in life? The answer is no. The primary purpose of the Sabbath is to enact an appointed time of weekly healing and growth for the *nefesh*, *ruach* and *neshama*.

The joy or zeal that we bring to our relationships on both axes mends the fragmentation of self and soul that has torn and vexed our sense of wellbeing. After all, doesn't the conflict between what we feel and how we act form the basis of a lot of mental illness? Sigmund Freud taught us that a person is composed of three elements; id, superego and ego. The tension between superego and id will create the structure of the ego. The extent to which that tension with the superego and id cannot be resolved, results in neurosis. Freud employed his psychoanalytic terminology to make the same point that is being made here. We need to strive for a wholeness of self, a full and complete embracing of our ability to be filled with zeal, wonder and awe. Compartmentalizing or ignoring part of our self is not healthy.

Attending to our zealousness; allowing ourselves to feel and express the sheer joy of life and love and incorporate what we feel into our whole person, allows us to unite the self, soul and spirit.

From the Bible: God wants to give us the greatest gift - His presence in our lives; to feel connected to the One. That is why we are commanded, "To love the Lord your God, listen to the Voice and bond to Him because God is your life" (Deut 30:20). What reason would there be for God to want to bond with us? Is the Celestial One that needy? Is He in dire want of companionship, praise? It is an oxymoron to say that God is incomplete. Therefore, by definition, God needs nothing. How then can the Omniscient, Omnipotent One be so limited as to need to bond with us? What is the meaning of the commandment to be connected to God?

The key to deciphering the biblical phrase is "Because God is your life." That is, you should love God because the life force that seeks release is that openness to feel wonder and zeal. In other words, the Text is revealing the secret to feeling the vitality of existence flow through your veins. Here is the opportunity to open a window, the Bible indicates, and unfetter the very meaning of life. "Because God is your life" is the answer to the most vexing question of being alive: 'How do I achieve joy?' Every fiber of your being becomes whole when freed from the confines of the stricture of inhibition to feel and express love. Loving God becomes synonymous with achieving selfhood.

We learned earlier, "You who are bonded with the Lord, your God, are alive, fully, today" (Deuteronomy, 4:4). The more connected we feel to God the more alive we become. The closer we are to the Source, the more we feel the current with the Foundation of All Things coursing through us. The vertical and the horizontal planes are required to awaken the reaches of the self: It is all connected. At the fulcrum of these two planes stands the ultimate goal of every person. Wholeness.

In Genesis, just before the unleashing of the waters of the Flood, the Bible says that God was "saddened in His heart." Can Perfection be disappointed? Can the Holy One really be sad? One ancient commentator named Sforno explained that God becomes sad when we deprive ourselves of meeting our potential. Isn't the greatest disappointment of a parent when their offspring have a gift, a talent, or an inheritance and they proceed to squander it? Instead of using their endowment, they ignore it and chase ephemera. Isn't that a tragedy? A terrible waste? Could it be the One also feels that we have mis-spent our unique bequest? That we are not interested in receiving the present He wants to give us?

We pursue the fleeting: We salivate over more money, exotic cars, designer homes, fancy clothing, sex and power; things which provide a momentary whiff of joy. Can the pursuit of these things cause an abiding, raw pain for God? As the old saying goes, "More than the baby wants to suck, the mother wants to nurse." When a baby refuses to nurse from its mother, the mother experiences an in-tense emotional and even physical pain. So it is with God. While the chasm of the soul might be bridged by incorporating more love, feeling and expressions of hope in our life, another stream of Divine Love is coming out to meet ours.

In the Bible, there are many references to sacrifices. Not many people besides scholars realize though that the Hebrew word for sac-rifice *korban*, has its etymology in 'to draw close.' The prime objec-tive of the rites of Temple sacrifices was to find a metaphysical place to come close to God.

Simon bar Yohai, author of the Zohar, said "I was bound to Him with a knot". Elsewhere in the same mystical work, Simon Bar Yo-hai says, "My soul was united to Him, burning for Him." Could this be the real intent of the sacrifices flaming on the altar of long ago? Were the offerings a symbol to later generations that we are sup-posed to tend the fires of emotion and allow them expression? The inner fires of the soul also need stoking. Those smoldering embers give rise to fires that afford us the opportunity to jump across the emotional barrier to wholeness.

Let's review: Novocain is good for the dentist's chair, not as a standard tool for navigating through life. We do not require any fur-ther anesthetization from living. We need to be aware of the joy that inheres in the mundane as well as the profound. In the former, I am reminded of an old preacher who quoted a farmer who said, "I al-ways put on my glasses before I eat strawberries and, thank the Lord, they become so much more large and luscious that way!" We can dull the experience of life or put magnifiers on our eyes to enhance the impact.

Jonathan M. Case

To first realize and appreciate all that exists in and around us is of paramount importance is a powerful force for change. Everything proceeds from the simple and fans outward in a myriad of forms. Love gives birth to love. Joy leads to joy. In the second instance, to stand in awe of the universe; to look up to the heavens as the jaw hangs wide and exclaim, "Who is the Author of all this?" (Zohar) is an expression of infinite sublimity.

A fire burns within. It is akin to the flames that once roared inside the Holy Temple of Jerusalem of old. This internal fire, like that old one, is a conduit to God. Feeding the fire allows the flames of the soul to loom large and allow all three aspects of the self to become open, receptive and whole. At the same time, the horizontal expressions of exuberance, joy and connection are also powerful connections to the world. What makes us feel good and complete is when we can laugh, pray and dance to the tune of our soul.

Chapter 5

An ennobled self

The venerable sage Rabbi Simon peered at the holy text from Exodus 15 and read: "Who is like You among the mighty?"

He then turned his bright eyes towards his acolytes and taught them the true meaning of the verse, "Come and look at what is really meant here: When the Holy Temple was built below, it was only based upon Judgment....This is because this is the place [the Temple] where Judgment resides. In another time, the Holy One, blessed be He, shall build it on a different, higher plane and it will be based not on Judgment, but Righteousness. That is why the great prophet Isaiah says: "In righteousness You will be established" (54:14). *This* [Temple] will endure and shall never be destroyed."

--Zohar

M uch of this book (and what we learn throughout the passage of our years) is that perception colors how we see the world. How we react to those patinas and interact with them is a reaction to that perception. A simple illustration; for one person, a forest can be foreboding, full of lurking dangers that wait, fangs extended, in the deep shadows. That same forest to another person can be a whimsical, fairy-like place where we can lose our selves in a lush, fragrant garden. They are the same place. What is the real difference between them? The mind dictates how we interpret what we see. The truth of the mind becomes the truth of reality. This idea is charged with much possibility. Knowing that we construct and are welded to our reality is a great realization; it is a leap of imagination which can be turned into strength.

What is so essential about knowing that we choose our own reality? What is the real significance to understanding that the way we view life is important? Does it really empower us? How does it make us strong?

Accepting that the way which we perceive the world can translate that perception into a reality which gives us control over the universe that spirals around us. Using the above example, knowing that the forest is a foreboding place will make us cautious. Knowing that the forest is where we find serenity will yield that end. Perception is a choice. Reaction proceeds from perception.

When we accept the reality of the mind, we become transformed from victims or passive bystanders of events into active participants in the play of life. The ability to control our destiny and live to our potential becomes manifest. We are empowered. Being aware of the power of perception and how we parlay that into reality, we become beings who finally wield control over our lives and fate.

To live a good life is a choice. Just as our view of the forest is a choice, so too is our view of life. Life can be a malignancy where the best we can hope for is to not get sick. On the other side, life can be abundant opportunity for exploration, awe and love. A person who wants to walk with God will want to make choices of perception that allow them to be come filled with goodness.

Sometimes attitude is not sufficient. There are times when we do not feel 'good' or kind. There are moments when we lose our patience and seethe and boil with rage. Have we then lost control of our ability to be in command of our self? Does it mean that the great strength that we hold has been forfeited? Have we lost the battle? Has this whole exercise been for naught? An utter waste of time and we would have been far better getting a massage...

The ultimate question is not whether we can be good when we are well fed, the savings account holds steady, when the kids are behaving and all else is going fine but whether we can be good when events are not going the way we would like them to go.

I have often seen the bumper sticker "Practice random acts of kindness." When I get around to printing my bumper stickers I will remove "random." Why should goodness be only random? We should we be kind only when we feel moved to be kind? Can't we also be good when we do not feel particularly disposed to be beneficent? In fact, now that I think about it, I will take out "Practice" too and in its place substitute "Do." Why *practice* being kind? Is it wise to experiment with goodness instead of allowing it to become part of the fabric of our self? My bumper sticker will simply read "Do kindness."

Deeds exert a strong influence on attitude. The reality that we perceive can often be created by the deeds we perform.

There is a phrase in the Bible that has caused scholars throughout the long stretches of millennia no end of discussion and argument. It states, "Love the Lord your God." Why should this terse, elegant phrase be the cause of so much hubbub? Isn't it absolutely obvious? Love God. Simple. Actually, it is not so clear at all. Think of the problems that arise: What if a person doesn't love God? What if they are angry at Him? What if they can't love God? Does that make them a bad person? Incapable of ever meeting God's grace? Does God need our love?

The way of love, the ancients declared, is the way of life. This is the energy that drives us. It is also a truism that sometimes love states one thing while actions may convey an entirely different message. Our mouths may speak of love but if actions are not in harmony with the words, the words are lies. We are defined by what we do with our hands and our feet. Who cares if your wife tells you she loves you and then has an affair with another man? Who cares if your parents deliver long speeches about their care and nurturing but are not present when the world closes in on you and desperation mounts? What difference does it make if a presidential candidate tells us he is in favor of helping the poor but only makes tax cuts for the rich? Words are meaningful only when they are true. The demonstration of truth is when our actions blend neatly with what we say.

That is why the wise ones of long ago spoke of God as a 'Commander.' There can be no 'commander,' they argued, unless there is a 'commandee.' Understanding who we are in relation to God is shown by the way that we accept the dicta of the Commander. Our fidelity or love is shown by action, not just the word. This is the ultimate path of loving God. The wizened sages uniquely taught that the way to love God is to demonstrate that love by realizing the relationship that inheres in the space between heaven and earth. Words of love alone are meaningless. Actions are the colors of the painter. They give articulation and depth to the painting. In the vast space created by the Maker, waiting to be filled, we are given the opportunity of a life to embody the principles of love.

Can we see faith? If you saw a Mother Theresa, would you recognize her intrinsic faith? Her goodness? That is, would she look like a saint? Or would we pass by her without a sideways glance, this feeble old woman draped in a plain cloth? Can you *see* goodness?

Goodness is only observable by the movement of our hands and feet. Love is demonstrable by deed, not word. So could you recognize Mother Theresa on the street? If you were paying attention to the care she would shower on the ones who were shunned by others, yes! What are the tell-tale marks of an Oskar Schindler? When he saw suffering he was immediately moved to assuage that pain. It would not be difficult to see such acts of altruism because they are tangible. There is no empirical evidence for love, just acts of kindness which is the greatest evidence of the existence of love. Saints do not necessarily look like saints but they act like it. Those acts have a direct correlation to what we think of ourselves.

Not long ago I found myself debating some high school students in a class I was teaching about the world of politics. We began talking about the United States and its interventionist stand in the world. Most of the students strongly felt that the United States ought to leave the rest of the world alone. "Why should we get killed for them? It is not like they asked us to invade their country anyway," said one. Another voice declared, "What they do with their own people is their business and we should mind our own affairs." "We have enough problems right here."

Then, I asked, "If you were walking down the street and someone was getting beaten up by a bunch of bullies, what would you do?" The answer I expected back did not come. The students agreed that it was not their business and that they should walk away before they get pulverized.

"And what if that person being beaten was you?" I asked.

A few years back I was exiting off a highway in suburban New York when my car began to wobble violently. I braked and pulled over to find out what was causing the car to raggedly veer and bounce dangerously. In the grassy center of the ramp I discovered it was a flat rear tire. It was not an unpleasant day and since I had no cell phone, all I could do was wait, until help arrived.

I waited. Many cars zoomed by as their drivers and passengers craned their necks to peer at me.

One half hour.

It was a long wait and in my boredom I began to gaze back at the people who were so curious about me. There was little else to do than fantasize about where they were going and what they were thinking as they drove by staring at me.

One hour.

By now I was getting impatient as I was hoping one of the people passing me might offer to call a tow truck or ask if I needed help. Maybe with a little luck someone I knew might pass by.

Two hours.

Finally twenty minutes later, a police car stopped and radioed for assistance.

I reckon that several hundred cars passed by me on that afternoon. And I wondered where all those cars with the bumper stickers were when I needed them, "Practice Acts of Random Kindness?" It is indeed a sad world where each person is so cut off from one another that we would rather observe someone in distress (perhaps uttering a brief prayer that we did not suffer that indignity) than risk personal intervention. This, as they say, is "where the rubber meets the road."

Goodness and love are not ideas to the religious mind: If it were only a notion, it would be a lie. It would ultimately cease to exist. Goodness, kindness and love may *start* with an idea but needs to be actualized so that it breathes and lives. Once practiced with regularity, acts of the hands translates back to the mind and becomes cemented into the fabric of our being. That is why saints are recognizable as saints; they behave that way.

This is also why I would erase those words from that bumper sticker. It is far more important to be kind all the time, even if we do not feel like being kind. In fact, might it be more important to be a generous spirit *especially* when we do not feel so inclined? I suspect this is true because our actions form our opinions, and not necessarily vice versa. How we behave is converted into how we feel about ourselves and the world. Back to an idea raised earlier in this chapter, what does it mean to 'love God?'

The Zohar quote at the start of this chapter spoke of the Temple in Jerusalem being erected of stones of Judgment. What the holy Master had in mind when he uttered those words was that the greatest, most awesome place on earth was constructed of stricture, commandments. These were the foundation stones of the Temple. The Temple was not made out of love. It could not be cast from love because before there is that kind of intense connection, there must first be an understanding of the boundaries of that relationship. Love is not the starting point; it comes as a result of an established relationship of mutual responsibility. Put another way, had the Temple been made from Love instead of Judgment it would have swiftly collapsed because humanity would not have done its part to hold it up. Without the girders of our efforts, the building would have fallen away. Actions lead to emotion.

Yes, God wants us to love Him, but to get to that emotional level is to first understand that the starting place of that love is how we behave. It is far easier to simply build our Temple out of love and skip the first step of sweat, effort, failure and triumph. Behavior informs the depth of what we feel. It does not necessarily work the other way around.

Just because we feel love, it does not follow that we will act with righteousness. I am confident that most, if not all, the people that passed me the day of my flat tire felt bad for me. They empathized. I imagine that people turned toward one another in their cars as they saw me stranded and said things like, "poor guy." Or, "I hope someone comes soon." They were people of good intent. Yet, the intent did not translate into behavior. Had they stopped and offered help, *and not felt anything toward my plight*, a wellspring of righteousness would eventually pursue and become a part of their persona.

Gradually, after the seeds of mutual responsibility have been planted in a sustained relationship, they blossom into love. The Temple was only built in the belief that any relationship begins with an understanding of where the boundaries and responsibilities lie.

But the Zohar quietly delivers a second message to the alert reader that is searching for that which is hidden. God does not want us to build the ethereal Temple edifice for His sake; His desire is for us to construct it for our sake. The mystical passage intimates that it is good for us to erect this Temple with the works of our hands. God does not need it, we do. The meaning of this is that we can neither employ others to do our work nor can we use the building that our forbears created. Each structure bears our name alone.

We have arrived at a very sacred place. Our personal Temple, our spiritual sanctuary, is built on deeds. Doubts are smoothed and erased through our good actions. Self-recrimination languishes when we cast a life of kindness. Unlike the commonly held beliefs that if we live in the moment, or learn to let go of past pain or hold fast to a great notion of how to live an enriched life (all of which are true), the way of Kabbalah commences with an understanding of the whole self and God and how our actions inform that relationship. We are defined by what we do. Mother Theresa was who she was because of what she did. So, too, with Gandhi, King or Mandela. Sainthood is not always recognized and rewarded. The satisfaction is all soulful.

Why must we do the tedious and menial work of construction? Growth is goal-oriented. If we desire a connection with God; if we hunger for a feeling of emotional stability and spiritual health; if we seek meaning from our lives it requires effort. Kabbalah represents the opportunity for the consummate growth of the soul. We are what we do. Just as profound is that we arrive at self-definition by what we do. This is a critical idea. We have a upbeat opinion of ourselves when we like what we have done. Similarly, we have a negative self image when we do not approve of our deeds. Kindness is not -- and must not be -- random. That may be a trite and convenient path but random goodness does not nourish the hungry soul. Do we like ourselves? Are we happy when we gaze into an unfiltered mirror? What makes a positive self definition is that we like the things we have done.

At night, are you driven by nightmares? In the daytime does a dark shadow intrude upon an otherwise bright day and cause harsh internal pain? Are there days when you just feel inadequate? Or have you become enraged at little gnat-like annoyances that make no sense? We may wonder, 'Why do I feel so distraught?' 'Why does life appear so dismal and dark?'

Here lies great wisdom from this passage in the Kabbalah: We like ourselves when we behave in a way that makes us proud. We feel happy when we know we are acting in consonance with God. A strong sense of positive self-esteem looms large and connects the three parts of the self- *nefesh, ruach* and *neshama*- when we recognize our place as 'commandee' and the Holy One as the 'Commander.' It is then that our life makes sense. We know why we are alive and that our existence makes a difference: whether we are alive or dead is of consequence. We matter. That path of goodness may not make us rich or even popular, but we will respect who we are, we will like what we have become because we admire the Temple we have created.

Is this what Rabbi Simon has been trying to tell us? Only after the Temple of Judgment has been constructed; only after we have made an effort with and lived in the edifice we have built and have learned to take our responsibilities seriously are the stones of that house then converted to the Temple of Righteousness. The first structure is crafted by us through effort; the second is gifted to us by God when we have made the first movement; when we have earned it.

There is a single episode that is related in an old text about the Exodus from Egypt worth reading for its powerful import. The story is told when the Children of Israel, having arrived at the shores of the Sea of Reeds, were confronted with an impenetrable body of water in front and waves upon waves of Egyptian warriors dispatched by the Pharaoh to annihilate them at their rear. The people seeing their doom rise all around them begin to shout and moan and cry. They beg their leader. They plead with Moses to take them back and save them from this certain death. Moses, too, is bewildered. Confused, Moses looks to the people and then prays to God for salvation. Nothing happens. God turns away from Moses' petition and the people's helplessness. The drone from below becomes frenzied as the people's voices turn to utter anguish seeing nothing happen.

At that moment a previously unknown man, Nachshon, steps forward into the waters of the Sea and wades up to his neck. Only then do the waters divide so that the Israelites can venture into the realm of their freedom. Moral? Change happens but not without first wading up to our neck and feeling the waters gather around, pressing us toward the greatest personal change.

A tale: On Passover night it is a commandment to tell the age-old story of Liberation from bondage. A great teacher and his pupil were caught in the maelstrom of Nazi Poland not so long ago. Both men were arrested and taken to the Gestapo Headquarters in Warsaw.

SS guards hit them and then, for their sadistic delight, decided to provide an opportunity for some further gratuitous suffering. They threw the two into a cell with a heartless thief wanting to see the criminal beat up and bloody the two Jews. The thief went immediately to work pushing the old one around the cell, cursing and punching.

The aged teacher felt the terrible blows against his face and body and turned to the thief and gazed at him incredulously, "Why are you hurting me? I didn't put you in here. I am suffering just like you." The thief stopped, looked around and then turned away.

When it became quiet and the thief rested in a corner, the elder turned to his young acolyte and said, "You know what this night is. It is the holy night for telling the story, the ancient tale of Freedom. It is a commandment. We must begin." The younger man wept, "Master, I cannot. I lost my family today. Everything is gone. My home. My life. I cannot do it. I cannot."

Listening from his corner was the thief. He lifted his head and asked what they were talking about. The Teacher told him that evening was the anniversary of the great Liberation from enslavement. It was a commandment to share that particular story in every generation on the sacred night. "If your friend won't listen, tell me the story," said the thief.

So began the master relating the ancient tale from Hebrew translating it into Polish word for word, sitting with the thief, telling the full story until four in the morning.

The thief made that night possible: He transformed that profane place into a pocket of timeless holiness because without his willingness to question and be engaged, there could have been no tale, no remembrance, no Seder.

The SS guard returned eager to see what had happened to the three men in the cell. He saw the old teacher and the thief deep in conversation. Enraged, the guard took them outside and shot them.

The younger man survived that hell. After the war, he told Shlomo Carlebach this story.

The purpose of life is not life. The purpose of life is purpose.

And the greatest purpose is the pursuit of righteousness.

The Temple erected from Judgment is erected in each generation, in every epoch, by every person. That Temple was not an event that occurred once in history. Throughout life we were exposed many times to this building, told of its power and meaning. The tale and meaning is repeated in each person's life countless times until they get it, own the vision, or die without ever acknowledging it. The transformation from the one Temple into the other needs to be accomplished by every person. It is only upon those stones of understanding that the ultimate foundation stones are laid, the stones of Righteousness.

When we feel generous it is easy to be charitable. On the other side, what happens when we feel tired, abused or empty? Sure, it is easy to be full of joy and hope when all goes well... but what about the other days? To put this question in a more personal way, "How can I turn my life into a sacred life?" How can we separate out what is vital from what is meaningless tripe? Is it possible to live a life that is fully engaged by the moment while living with an ennobled sense of self?

Yes.

When we have learned and attenuated our personhood to taking seriously the existence and importance of the Temple of Judgment and acting as if every moment were the moment we were created for, we achieve that height of meaningful existence. Sure, there are times when we do not feel charitable or kind. There are times when the dark cloud over our head seems to penetrate every fiber of our body. Still, the life that acknowledges the validity of another person's needs is a life ennobled.

Most times, the other person at the stop sign can go before us. We can usually hold the door open for the elderly. We have enough energy to compliment someone on their appearance most of the time. We have enough money to give our loose change to the needy. There is enough space in our life to practice acts of goodness countless times each day. That is enough to shift the dark clouds away and allow rays of light to penetrate our being. Unless we are in an ambulance, it is safe to assume that life and death are not part of our day. We have time enough.

The same is true of faith. Every religion demands its adherents to nourish their relationship to God thereby encouraging you in the process the building of your first Temple. Find it. Do it. Let that become a "religious" behavior all day long, all life long (Remember that the word 'religious' means *consistent* as in "brush your teeth religiously.").

Caveat:

Until we learn to do good things just because they are good, we may well sabotage our next step to serving God out of a sense of *devekute*, the embrace of the Divine. 'What's the point,' we may think, 'of believing in God, much less following Him, if I am not blessed (read: rewarded) for the good things I do?' The expectation that we will be thanked, rewarded, given a raise, promotion or some other accolade will lead us down that dark and confining Road of Despair. As the holy Talmud states, "Serve the Master without thought of reward."

Let us review what we have learned. The most noble kind of life begins with a love that is created from a relationship with God. Such love is predicated upon accepting the terms of a relationship that is both ongoing and consistent. While we may not always feel loving, our actions have enough power in them to change the course of how we feel.

The tripartite aspects of the soul, *nefesh*, *ruach* and *neshama*, requires nourishment. They must not be starved. Our soul needs to be continually fed just like our body. What is the food of the soul? Not acting out of self-interest and self-aggrandizement but out of goodness. Once we have made a regular feature of acting in accord with God, our life is catapulted from 'trying to invent a reason to be alive' to the universe of the sublime where every action is laden with meaning.

The terms of this engagement are simple and self-evident. We already know them to be true. Every day people attempt to gather the reason for their life and act upon it with abandon. That is why entrepreneurs are so zealous in their marketeering. The same is true for race car driving, running, drinking, sexual conquests, investments.... Eating makes us all feel good but as the aphorism goes, "We eat to live; we do not live to eat." A universal truth is that there must be a reason for our existence. It is why any person throws energy into any act which they have come to believe will endow their days with satiety and a feeling of accomplishment. While we create many varied reasons for being alive, there is only one universal and timeless truth of existence.

The soul knows the real goal. It has known the truth all along. The short, immediate goals of life that allows us to prosper are not what makes life worthwhile. They simply make it possible for us to survive. What endows our days with ultimate meaning is when we access the needs of our soul, our higher self, and then nourish them. Our task is then to waken the lower parts of the self to that same realization.

People need a reason for being alive, a meaning. Such reason will filter into our waking and slumbering moments. It will penetrate each cell of our self and fill it. The goodness we do will provide a framework for all that we do but, more importantly, it will provide a self-definition. We will know who we are, why we were born, where we stand in the universe and the value of our life. Only then do we stand the greatest chance to develop into a master of the self. That is the absolute source of well-being.

Section Three

And the Moral of the Story Is...

It is written in Genesis , "A river comes out of Eden to water the garden and from there [Eden], it was parted" (2:10). This indicates that the river, which is the generative aspect of the Almighty, comes out of Eden, representing Wisdom, one of the higher spheres of God. The river then enters the Garden which represents the kingship of God to water it [the Garden] from the Supernal waters and brings it rich nutrients allowing it to produce both fruit and seed. This gives delight to all. The Garden is pleased with its fruit, which brings pleasure to the river, because it made the fruit.... Rabbi Elazar expounded: This is the secret of the matter of the river which comes out of Eden - only the river, which is one of the lowest elements of God produces offspring, and without it, no other aspect can produce fruit.

-- Zohar

Examining something as trivial as the physical aspects of Eden, Kabbalah misses nothing. Everything has multiple meanings extracted from its many rich layers. Often, a hidden purpose can only be revealed by the person who possesses the right mindset and depth of learning. A Kabbalistic premise: If the Bible is a holy document, nothing is extraneous. No word or even vowel of the Text is without meaning. The only question is, are we wise enough to grasp the significance?

That which has the appearance of uselessness always has meaning. Everything matters. No matter how sordid, random or trite the event, everything is more than it appears. Each chance meeting is not a chance. Every interaction holds great treasures within its hidden vaults. Yet, they are of no value to us unless we first open them and peer inside. "Do not look at the exterior," warns an ancient text. It goes on to say that there are new beautiful casks which hold rancid wine and ancient unattractive casks which hold an elixir.

That kind of understanding requires an awareness of the preciousness that inheres in every person, each encounter. We are immeasurably enriched by every encounter when we are awake. Everything, everyone and even time is holy. A moment is a teacher of infinite and irreplaceable value. It only happens once. There are no "repeat performances." To be awake for each meeting ought to be a major concern, for it will never recur: that connection has never happened since the inception of the universe and will never happen again through all time. And, it is just possible that if we are awake, we might be the unwitting, and yet indispensable, messenger who sets in motion a chain of events that could bring about the ultimate redemption. The Messiah is waiting down by the Gates of the Old City. If the appointment is missed, our state of sleep could bring doom.

Being awake/aware of every meeting means that we will consciously treat each circumstance for what it is: "This has never happened before. Since the beginning of time, I am the first to be here." That is all. With such an utterance and expectation, light suffuses every meeting.

A Tale:

It used to be that weddings in Europe were lavish affairs where every member of the community was invited. From the wisest to richest to the downtrodden poor, everyone was to be included in the wonderful events surrounding the binding of two souls. Once there was to be one such great wedding in the village of Annapol.

The head of the community, of course, was among the honored guests but was dismayed to find that his name was listed third on the list of the invited guests. Irritated at this slight, he arrived late and was, therefore, seated on the side furthest from the bride and groom. Adding more insult to his pride, by the time the food he was served to him, it was cold. He rose from his seat angrily and left the wedding disgruntled.

A sage, Zusia, whose name appeared last on the same list, arrived early, ready to fulfill the important religious commandment of rejoicing with the bride and groom. Because Zusia was so early, he was seated right next to the groom, an auspicious place of honor. Then Zusia was served a hot delicious meal because of his placement and was among the first to dance in the long celebrations that lasted throughout the night.

Zusia became so excited by all this wondrous celebration and his fortune that he called out to God, "Dearest Father, You are the Groom and we are the bride!" In this state, Zusia danced out of the hall and continued to dance all day and night until exhausted, he looked up to heaven, "Master of the Universe, Zusia is hungry and tired!"

When Zusia finally returned to town, he met the leader who was so insulted by the party listing him third, then seating him so far from the place of honor and giving him cold food. He gazed at Zusia and asked, "How could you have such an overwhelming, ecstatic experience at the same wedding which I did not enjoy at all?"

Zusia answered, "My teacher, you came expecting everything and received nothing. I came expecting nothing and I received everything."

Every moment is alive with possibility and meaning. Each of them bears something for us, just as we, too, are messengers that bear gifts to those whom we meet. No expectations. No preconceptions. Even children are teachers of life.

In fact, the Kabbalah often places in the mouths of children the greatest wisdom. But it is meaningless gibberish if we are inattentive and expecting them to utter nonsense. Children may impart great wisdom, but only if we are willing to be attentive to their teaching. Knowing all this to be true heightens each meeting and exponentially increases the odds that the gifts will be accepted and delivered to their ultimate destination.

Openness is the first key of Kabbalah. To be ready for each encounter with an eager attitude towards gleaning the richness of every experience opens the heart to God and humanity. These interwoven axis –horizontal and vertical --will prepare us for the greatest journey we will ever undertake. Untold wisdom and discernment lies in the simple act of becoming an open vessel. Nothing can enter when the bottle is stoppered. Open your heart.

The passage of life also commences with a realization that we are waiting for no one. We may be expecting the Messiah, but in the meanwhile we do not stop living and striving until his arrival. In the play, "Waiting for Godot," Samuel Beckett writes of a couple of friends, Didi and Gogo, who wait for their friend/savior to come to deliver them into their deserved light. They speak anxiously of the decisions that need to be made and numerous paths in front of them. When Godot arrives, they agree, he will settle all their problems. Godot will reveal the truth. The audience is gripped with impatience as we also wait to see what Godot will bring.

It is an arduous anxious-ridden play as the audience also wonders when this character will finally appear. In the end, he does not arrive. The play draws to a close while the audience is wondering if Godot even exists, let alone whether he will ever come! Didi and Gogo have waited in vain. The moral? Godot will not come to relieve our boredom, save us from oblivion, or provide the hidden answers to the deepest questions of life. Or he might come. Either way, we do not stop living a vital life. What will ultimately save us, imbue our days with meaning, is rediscovering the soulful fire that burns inside us. The sacred gift we were endowed with is the initial spark igniting our present and casting illumination on our future, waiting to be unleashed. It waits only for us.

'Letting go' is the primary key to receiving. Letting go of preconceptions and fixed, rigid ideas about the meaning of life releases us to God and one another. Full hands cannot hold more possessions. I have the image of a child let loose in a candy shop. As he desperately tries to stuff as many sweets as he can into his pants, shirt, his hat, the candies keep popping out because there is just too much of it jamming every free space on his body. How much do we really need? How much is enough?

While society has connived to convince us that "more is better", that kind of thinking betrays us and ultimately keeps us from having a soul that can be replenished. We can never have enough of anything. We will always leave the table hungry, desiring more. That is why emptying ourselves of expectations is so critical to absorbing the wise and mighty lessons of Kabbalah.

One final tale: Once upon a time there lived an irrepressible, holy and devout soul. He lived a beautiful life of giving, sharing. God took great delight in the man and the Celestial One smiled. So pleased by the exuberance with which he lived and the care he took in every step of his life that God decided to celebrate this man's life. The Almighty One came to the holy man and asked, "What can I give you, my precious son? What can I offer you as a gift for all your devotion and goodness?"

The man paused for a moment. Then he answered that the greatest gift he desired would be the opportunity to do many good deeds without ever knowing the outcome of those acts. God laughed.

And He said, "It is done."

It was such a wonderful wish that God gave it as a gift to humanity in perpetuity. Every person would be so blessed afterward. Our moment is now.

CPSIA information can be obtained
at www.ICGtesting.com
Printed in the USA
FFOW03n0908281214
9877FF